The HABIT *factor*®

An Innovative Method to
Align Habits with Goals to
Achieve Success

2ND EDITION

MARTIN GRUNBURG

EQUILIBRIUM ENTERPRISES, INC.

Library of Congress Cataloging-in-Publication data is available upon request.
ISBN: 978-0982050170

Grunburg, Martin A.

The Habit Factor®
An Innovative Method to Align Habits with Goals to Achieve Success

Second Edition: March 2015
Printed in the United States

Cover Design:
Equilibrium Enterprises, Inc. and "The Rock"

Volume discounts for educational, business and promotional sales use are available. Ask about our custom imprinted book-jacket service with your organization's logo. For bulk sales information, please email: **booksales@equilibrium-ent.com.**

Nobody improves the world without
first improving themselves.

10% of all author royalties are donated to children's not-for-profit organizations, primarily
Big Brothers Big Sisters of America and Junior Achievement.

Mentor • Educate • Inspire

Dedicated to <u>YOU</u>,
your success,
and many perfect days.

*"You cannot live a perfect day
without doing something for someone who will
never be able to repay you."*
~Coach John Wooden

"All men's natures are alike –
it's their habits that carry them far apart."
~Confucius, 500 B.C.

"Your net worth to the world is usually determined by what remains after your bad habits are subtracted from your good ones."
~**Benjamin Franklin, 1778**

"It makes no small difference to be habituated this way or that way straight from childhood, but an enormous difference, or rather all the difference."
~Aristotle, 342 BC

You likely noticed that each of the previous quotes rests on its own page. This is by design, as the wisdom contained within each deserves your *special* attention. It is no small coincidence that the wisest men of their representative cultures and generations had settled on a single, *identical* truth – a truth that governs each of our destinies. This truth might simply be known as The Habit Factor.

CONTENTS

CONTENTS

HABITS: THE INTERSECTION 95

HABITS: APPLICATION 142

CONTENTS

CONTENTS

PREFACE

It's a bit hard to believe that it has already been four years since the original release of The Habit Factor® book, and while I had hoped (and believed) this book would help people, I'm still a bit startled by the cumulative impact of the book and companion app after such a short period of time. As I wrote the book, I told myself that if it helped just one person it would be a worthwhile endeavor.

About three months after the book's publication, I was invited to speak at a TEDx conference in the United Arab Emirates. Shortly thereafter, a handful of top productivity blogs such as Mashable.com and Lifehacker.com featured The Habit Factor app, book or both. Southwest Airlines Magazine (of all publications) released a "Goal Getters" New Year's article that featured The Habit Factor, and Cigna – a billion-dollar healthcare provider – selected The Habit Factor as a top-rated health and well-being app for its curated Go-You Marketplace. Later, even The New York Times and C|Net Tech Minute showcased The Habit Factor app. Best of all, the coverage was unsolicited and, if nothing else, helped to reaffirm and validate the many ideas surrounding habit, productivity and goal achievement.

Since this is a book about habit and effective goal-setting, it's probably appropriate to share a quick tip and a funny story. I'm of the belief that you should keep your BIG goals quiet, really quiet, and share them with only a few of your closest friends (at most) and your spouse. I'm well aware that many "experts" will tell you to share your goals with as many people as possible; however, many of my reasons for advocating secrecy have been affirmed in a popular TED talk[1].

The gist is, you can waste a lot of energy running around telling people what you intend to do when, in essence, the best thing to do is get busy doing it! To reiterate this particular mindset, I will often share a favorite Henry Ford quote: "You can't build a reputation on what you are going to do."

The story goes like this: A good friend, we'll call him Gary (that's actually his name), became a bit angry when my book was released since he wasn't aware I had started to write a book in the first place. I explained to him that nobody essentially knew I was working on a book and went further to assure him that I didn't undergo the great pain of writing this (over three years) just to pull a fast one on *him*.

So, the moral of the story: Keep your goals quiet (very quiet) and be forewarned, should you accomplish them, your surprised friends may even become a little angry.

The Habit Factor became the first of its kind, a self-help book with a complementary mobile app empowering users to actually apply the ideas within the book. I wanted to ensure readers weren't left wondering, "OK, so how can I apply this info?" This can be a real challenge after completing most self-help books.

---

[1] http://www.ted.com/talks/derek_sivers_keep_your_goals_to_yourself?language=en

To that end, this edition goes even deeper into the practice of habit formation with an enhanced Application Plus section that leverages the additional four years of insight and experience I've garnered from presenting, coaching and holding workshops on this topic. Some readers, eager for action and change, may be tempted to jump straight to the Application section, but *please don't fall into that trap.* The ideas that drive the Why and the How behind The Habit Factor are critical to your eventual success. This includes the science and insight behind what makes The Habit Factor methodology work and will assist and inform your efforts immeasurably!

One of my many goals with The Habit Factor book was to help eliminate the erroneous negative connotation of "habit," replacing it with a more real and true understanding – the recognition that the fastest way to achieve your goals is via the intentional crafting and alignment of supportive habits.

If you were to take a quick survey of the personal development/self-help landscape today within iTunes or Amazon, for example, it would be impossible not to notice The Habit Factor's core message being amplified time and again with the proliferation of habit trackers and habit-development books, 99% of which did not exist prior to 2010.

That's the good news. The other news, unfortunately, is that many of these ebooks and apps are opportunistic (trying to capitalize on a trending subject matter), yet miss many key ideas, science and best practices surrounding habit development and goal achievement – perhaps most importantly *the critical relationship and distinction between goals and habits!*

It's often been said that when a person overcomes a great weakness, an even greater strength is born. For instance, many learning programs about language or reading have been created by people who dealt with challenges in those areas.

Reflecting now, I realize that it was my own frustration and inability to achieve some of my most important goals that gave birth to The Habit Factor, which in turn has helped so many others achieve their goals. This is extremely rewarding and at the same time very humbling.

I hope this message inspires you, as I'm *certain this is the methodology that will set you free from past struggles* no matter your prior level of frustration with goal achievement.

A few things you will find in this new, updated edition of The Habit Factor:

- Additional footnotes and edits
- Improved Kindle formatting
- Application tips and techniques, including some coaching tips
- A review of the P.A.R.R. methodology and HabitStrength™
- A detailed FAQ regarding many of the most frequently asked questions about topics from presentations, workshops and seminars

Toward the end of this book you'll also find a few essays from participants in The Habit Factor Challenge. Users were invited to track their habits for four weeks, submit their charts weekly via email (by a deadline), and then write an essay or compile a video (or both) about their Habit Factor experience. Their stories are great and I hope they embolden you to take action!

In the last chapter we've added some bonus material and a gift – a free invitation to join me at our new website via our latest cloud-enabled app[2], which will allow you to sync your habits, goals and tracking data across devices and ultimately across platforms. This is only the first iteration of the cloud app, and new features are already in the works.

In a world where there are hundreds of millions of books, I do not believe you've come upon The Habit Factor by chance. I suspect you bought this book for a reason: You believe you are capable of even more – no matter your current level of achievement.

So, metaphorically, I hand this book to you now with a smile, a small request and a hearty THANK YOU! My request is simple: Should we not cross paths in person, please share your success with me and the growing THF community via a book review, email, Twitter or Facebook!

May your journey be a much smoother one with The Habit Factor at your back!

With immense gratitude,

~Martin

---

[2] Depending upon when you read this, the "ProCloud" app may not yet be available; simply search "The Habit Factor" in your favorite app store.

THE HABIT FACTOR®

FOREWORD

Martin first contacted me via e-mail just after I had blogged about The Habit Factor® iPhone app. At the time, I had posted an entry about how my iPhone had become an integral part of my daily life, and how a handful of apps had become indispensable. I concluded the post by sharing that at the end of my day, I would reflect on my activities and check off those habits that were helping me get closer to achieving my goals.

Thereafter, we exchanged a few e-mails and he later invited me to write this Foreword. After reviewing The Habit Factor manuscript, I immediately recognized its significance and vital relevance to the challenges facing each and every one of us at this pivotal moment in human history. I wanted to do what I could to help this noble cause and spread this important message of awareness and inspiration, to help people dream bigger dreams and make them come true – and in so doing become more confident, happy and fulfilled. Not only did the message resonate with my own personal story of growth, but it also paralleled my own cause: to raise environmental awareness and understand the impact of our collective habits upon the world.

The first time I set out across an ocean – to row solo across the Atlantic in 2005 – I failed to truly appreciate the importance of The Habit Factor. Faced with unforeseen hardships, such as tendinitis in my shoulders, the breakage of all four of my oars within the first six weeks, and the highest frequency of storms ever recorded in the North Atlantic, I fell into a pit of despair and lost all motivation. Looking at the thousands of miles that lay before me, I was overwhelmed by the enormity of the challenge. I began skipping occasional rowing shifts, telling myself I could always make up for the lost efforts later.

The skipped rowing shifts became more frequent and my morale plummeted. The voices of self-doubt and self-criticism became louder as I fell further and further behind schedule.

Then one day, a moment of insight. I thought back to what had propelled me here in the first place. Only a few years earlier, I had reached a point of absolute desperation. I started seeking answers to some big questions. What did my life mean? What was the point of being me? But the question that really turned my life upside down was when I considered how I might be remembered. I sat down and wrote two versions of my own obituary – the one I wanted and the one I was headed for. They were very different; I realized I had to make some big changes if I was going to look back upon my life and be proud of my legacy.

That awareness now came back to me in my rowboat. I realized that I had lost focus on my goal and had become distracted by all the wrong things, the things beyond my control – the unexpected difficulties, the broken oars, the storms, the tendinitis, and so on. I recognized that if I was going to make it across the Atlantic successfully, I had to regain focus and take control of the here and now. I needed to do whatever I could at that moment to help me inch closer to my goal.

Since that moment, the principle of focusing on the process became my mantra, across the remainder of the Atlantic and the entire Pacific Ocean from California to Papua New Guinea, a distance of 8,000 miles. I held in my mind a very strong vision of how wonderful it would be to reach my destination – the warmth of the welcome; the first cold beer; the crisp white sheets of a clean, dry bed; and the white, fluffy towels after my first proper shower in three months. But I steadfastly refused to think about the almost incomprehensible number of strokes that I needed to take between where I was and where I wanted to go.

I'm excited for you. The book you hold in your hands and the techniques and insights within these pages will serve as a similar catalyst for your achievement and evolution. This book is practical, yet goes where no other book I've read before has gone. By delving into the realm of the intangible, you will learn about your powers of intuition, synchronicity and even the subconscious and how habit plays such a remarkable role. I'm impressed by this book because it doesn't promise to reveal any "secrets" and doesn't attempt to sell you anything other than a belief in yourself and your own abilities.

I am often asked how I manage to keep on going during these often difficult 100-plus-day journeys. My answer is fairly simple. If you have a big enough reason "why," you will always be able to find your "how." When I set out across the Atlantic, it was about much more than just the adventure. I was emerging from an old life that was materialistic, based on shallow values, and was ultimately unfulfilling both emotionally and spiritually. I purposefully wanted to reinvent myself as a person of influence, an adventurer, and planned to use my rowboat as a platform from which to share my newfound passion for sustainable living.

That passion is what keeps me heading out to sea, a habitat that I still find profoundly alien and endlessly challenging. Rather than trying to find "motivation" on a daily basis, which tends to lead to a tense, white-knuckled mental attitude, I find "inspiration" from nature and the possibilities of a greater future for our planet.

In mid-Pacific I had one more insight – the significance of habits not just personally, but in relation to our planet collectively. As the swirling area of plastic trash known as the North Pacific Garbage Patch grows to twice the size of Texas, as the amount of CO_2 in the atmosphere approaches 400 parts per million, as the rainforests are decimated year after year, it occurred to me that most of our problems are NOT the result of major catastrophes, but rather the accumulation of billions of tiny, careless acts. One plastic bag at a time, one unnecessary car ride, one tree that might have been saved – each mindless action we take daily as consumers and producers casts a vote for the kind of future we want for our world. However, when I look at the positives, I know that if we choose responsible decisions rather than careless ones, the condition can still reverse itself. The road is long, but I'm confident we can get there by making consistent, responsible and ethical decisions day after day, year after year – one decision at a time.

Individually and collectively, physically and emotionally, spiritually and ecologically, the world we create is really nothing other than a collective accumulation of our individual daily habits. It behooves each of us, in these times of great change, to step back and ask ourselves if our habits are taking us in the direction we desire to go, as individuals and as ambassadors of the only planet we have.

Enjoy this wonderful book.

Roz Savage
Ocean Rower
www.rozsavage.com

PROLOGUE

THE SHOWER HANDLE

I fixed our shower handle a couple of months ago. I had to – the pipe rusted on the inside of the wall and the handle fell off. The good news was, since it wasn't originally installed properly, this was my opportunity to correct the H and C designations. For more than five years, this has been a minor peeve. I figured it'd be nice if the H actually produced hot water and the C cold water. (Just as an aside, if you find yourself staying at the Mirage Hotel in Las Vegas, on the ninth floor, you may be lucky enough to enjoy the same concern.) So, after the shower handle was fixed, you'd expect my wife and me to be pretty pleased that it finally worked properly, right?

Well, consider that since we moved in, we had been "trained" to know that H equaled cold water and C produced hot water. Yes, we were literally programmed to expect that the H delivered cold water.

So, just yesterday, about mid-shower, I noticed the water getting too hot. I quickly and automatically without thought turned the handle to H again, programmed by my five years of use. Care to guess what happened?

Correct. I GOT BURNED! (Ouch.)

So, here's the question: How many of us are getting burned daily by our small (oftentimes very small) repetitive thoughts, actions and behaviors? How many of us are getting burned by our prior programming – by our automated responses? Simply put, how many of us are getting BURNED by our habituated responses on a daily basis?

It's interesting to me that this little episode actually took place while I was engaged in writing The Habit Factor and my awareness of my habits was already significantly heightened. But even my heightened awareness seemed to make little difference; my automated response simply took over. My neural wiring acted without me. My hand moved the handle without me even thinking about it.

The Habit Factor is about habits. However, it's also about climbing into the captain's chair of our subconscious, looking out over the horizon and identifying not just our life goals, but truly understanding and becoming highly aware of our current habits. It's about recognizing the incredible correlation between our own achievements and our habits.

In order to accomplish this, we are going to take a very deep dive into HABIT. In fact, I'd venture to guess this might be the deepest, most comprehensive and thorough analysis of habit, from multiple dimensions, there has ever been. Yes, I said *dimensions*. Believe it or not, the more I studied habit, the more I found that habits relate to so many different facets of our life, from psychology and biology to ecology and even astronomy, and seemingly everything in between.

While this analysis might become a little mind-bending at times, I can assure you that by the end of the book, you will never regard habit the same. And, if you apply just some of the understanding and techniques in this book, your achievement is certain to reach unprecedented levels.

TRY THIS

Quickly clasp your hands together with intersecting fingers (yes, put down the book please). Do that three times. My guess is that every time your fingers interlocked in the same manner, and more often than not (but not always), the dominant hand's pinkie is the lowest finger. Try this a few more times, and notice how the same result takes place naturally. Now, just for fun, try to clasp your hands with the opposite finger intersecting. Try to do that without thinking. How'd that feel?

You see, it's pretty apparent that we're literally wired for repetition. Everything we do physically (and mentally) involves energy; energy is pure and can be considered intelligent because it always seeks the simplest and most efficient route (think of water, a potent array of energy).

Every action we take is designed to be slightly easier the second time (this is why proper practice vs. just practice is so important). The term people often use for this is "muscle memory," again underscoring the fact that we are literally wired to remember. This is not a conscious remembering, but rather a subconscious recording that is stored for later reference.

WHY READ THIS BOOK?

"I don't have the discipline," or, "I'm just a constant procrastinator; I know what I need to do, but just don't seem to do it…"

Sound familiar?

Typically, the root causes of personal frustration, lack of fulfillment or even emptiness can be traced to one or both of the following: no clarity of purpose, or the notion that you aren't tapping into your potential. Simply put: You're not getting the most out of yourself and your abilities.

And, believe it or not, in many ways the key to all achievement is essentially the opposite of the classic Japanese proverb that says, "Beginning is easy, continuing is hard." Chances are you'll agree that getting started is the hardest part, and in fact, while never easy, continuing becomes easier – over time. It becomes easier because of a magical gift each of us have been endowed with – an extraordinary achievement device, a tool so powerful that it willingly performs the tasks you have programmed automatically and without conscious thought! Consider that for a moment … this remarkable gift, of course, is HABIT!

The true challenge, then, must be to bust through the initial resistance to literally begin moving – to break the inertia. This is absolutely essential. Procrastinators should recognize, much as Newton pointed out centuries ago, that "a body in motion tends to stay in motion," and therefore, "a body at rest will remain at rest." Certainly, if you've ever heard the saying, "When you want something done, then give it to a busy person," you can appreciate the truth in these observations.

In *The Republic*, Plato states, "The beginning is the most important part of the work." And, even though his context was in reference to a child's character, he states a simple truth, for without a beginning, there can be no end – no result. Therefore, it's worthwhile to keep in mind that you have little chance of doing something a second and a third time if you haven't done it yet a first time. This may sound a bit ridiculous, but the message cannot be overemphasized: You simply must get started, or, as Nike says, "Just do it®."

And, of course, The Habit Factor's corollary to Nike's famous slogan might be: "Just do it – *often*."

ENTER: THE CATALINA CLASSIC

"We do not try things because they are hard;
they are hard because we do not try them."

~Seneca

It was early February 2003, shortly after my 35th birthday, and I had a fairly unusual conversation. It was peculiar because it was a conversation I had with myself. Since the age of about 17, I'd heard about an almost mythical paddleboard race called the Catalina Classic. Participants paddled from Catalina Island to Palos Verdes and then up the coast to the Manhattan Beach Pier, which represented the finish line. In all, it was 32 miles across the unpredictable ocean channel stretching between Catalina Island and Los Angeles.

When I first heard about the event, I was completely captivated by it. Thirty-two miles! Are you kidding me? Paddling on your chest for the better part of a day, on a tiny board 14 feet long and about 20 inches wide. Do people really do this? Could I do this? I recall seeing the smiling faces filled with accomplishment in the surf magazines and the photos of those competitors who were completely exhausted, yet overjoyed. I remember thinking, "Someday I *have to* try that."

Before I knew it, years had passed and the event was a distant memory if it was a memory at all. Then, on my 35th birthday I found myself performing a "bucket-list" type of exercise. What experience would I totally regret not doing if

I died tomorrow? That question sparked a most peculiar answer: the Catalina Classic!

"Are you serious?" I tried to snap myself out of it. "You don't even own a paddleboard and you've never even paddled in *any* event, not one mile, not seven miles, and definitely not 32 miles! Do you have any idea how much training you'll have to do? You don't have the time for that! You have a family, business concerns and a host of other responsibilities."

However, there it was – undeniable, at the top of the list. By the way, you know it's a great goal if the first thing that happens is you get butterflies and you start making excuses or trying to rationalize exactly why you can't do it. Trust me when I tell you I had seemingly hundreds of excuses for not trying, but not one good reason.

"If not now, when?" The Catalina Classic had always been a "someday I'll give that a try" experience. The problem was my "somedays" were drying up. This was clearly an event that favored youth. "Now or never," I threatened. "Commit now or forget about it forever!" This produced a crucible-type moment, a moment I will never forget.

Before me lay a fundamental decision presenting two radically different outcomes: I could choose to challenge myself or I could simply do nothing and remain within my comfort zone – a path certain to provide no growth.

Next thing I knew, I was looking up all the information I could find about the event on the Internet. I noticed I could register for the annual event online, as well. I did not contemplate the decision any longer. Before I knew it, I'd received a congratulatory receipt via e-mail. I'd paid the

$150 or so for the entry fee, and that was it. The event was August 24, and I was now an official participant. I was shocked by the commitment. It was already mid-February, and I reminded myself that I didn't even own a paddleboard. I had my work cut out for me and had to begin planning my training immediately. I knew literally nothing about the sport of paddleboarding.

The learning curve was steep – very steep. To give you an idea, initially I literally couldn't paddle 10 feet without falling off my new board. The balance these boards demanded was like nothing I'd ever paddled on before – this was no surfboard. However, I was committed to my goal – probably more because of the fear of embarrassment that would have come from quitting than the thrill of completion.

Later (in the Application section) I will share a few of the many challenges I encountered during my training. While each setback was discouraging, each undoubtedly made me better for the effort, both physically and mentally stronger.

The short story, for now, is that on August 24 of 2003, I successfully crossed the finish line of the Catalina Classic at the Manhattan Beach Pier; the event took me seven hours, 22 minutes and 30 seconds. I was exhausted, but I was even more elated. Not because I broke any speed records, but because I'd finished what initially appeared improbable if not impossible.

The methodology I used to successfully complete the Catalina Classic eventually evolved into The Habit Factor. I decided to test the same process a few years later, and used it to successfully complete an Ironman-distance triathlon with no prior triathlon or even running experience. In fact, when I signed up, I did not even own running shoes or a road bike. And, for the Ironman-distance event, I had purposely limited myself to only nine months of training.

Before you think, "Well, good for you, you're some accomplished athlete," let me assure you that when I began my training, at 35 years old, I was no athlete. I probably thought I was, but after my initial training sessions I quickly realized just how out of shape I really was. At best, I was a weekend warrior who, if lucky, surfed once or twice a week.

A more realistic picture of me at the time is that of a desk jockey, working upwards of 60 hours a week. I had almost no balance in my life. The Habit Factor brought me immediate balance by shifting my personal energies (thoughts, emotions, behaviors) *in small increments, daily*.

Rest assured I don't share this story to impress you. I share the experience *only because it is largely responsible for the development of The Habit Factor*. In fact, both of these personal challenges helped to formulate many of the ideas within this book. It is also worth noting that these ideas and the supportive methodology are responsible for me achieving more meaningful accomplishments in the last seven years of my life than in the first 35 combined.

Finally, since I undertook each of these goals from a starting point of zero (no base knowledge or prior experience), ***I'm confident that you, too, can do the same with any goal you're passionate about achieving***.

In fact, this methodology has now been successfully applied around the world and has received some extraordinary praise from top trainers, personal development coaches and even PhDs. We regularly receive e-mails from people all over the world sharing the powerful impact this simple, innovative and practical methodology has had on their lives. Just a few days ago, a thoughtful e-mail arrived from a man in Slovakia who wrote to share some thoughts on the mobile app version of The Habit Factor methodology, and ended with, "I love your app, it has already changed my life so thanks."

```
>> Anyway i love your app, it has allready changed my life so thanks. I
>> hope my feedback would help to improve it
>>
>> Have a great day
>>
>> Martin from Slovakia
```

This sort of unsolicited feedback and praise is both exciting and humbling. Please know that I'm equally excited and humbled by the prospect of this book and methodology serving you.

The following pages explore HABIT (not as a singular word but as a profound concept) and reveal with great intensity both the "why" and the "how" behind the extraordinary force of habit. In fact, to fully grasp The Habit Factor's essence is to understand its *two distinct levels*: First, the surface level: It is an innovative and practical methodology for goal achievement via the creation, alignment and tracking of habits that are aligned to a goal. Second, the esoteric level: The Habit Factor explores exactly why habits exist and why they wield such influence upon our lives. At this deeper level, habit is explored and presented as a *language of creation and achievement,* one that requires *harmony* and *alignment* of our personal energies

16

(thoughts and actions) for true effectiveness. When both of these levels are embraced, understood and, most importantly, *applied*, all of your efforts – all of your achievements – become more efficient and easier over time.

INTRODUCTION

It is very important that teachers should realize the importance of habit, and psychology helps us greatly at this point. We speak, it is true, of good habits and of bad habits; but, when people use the word "habit," in the *majority* of instances it is a bad habit which they have in mind. They talk of the smoking habit and the swearing habit and the drinking habit, but not of the abstention habit or the moderation habit or the courage habit. But the fact is that our virtues are habits as much as our vices.

All our life, so far as it has definite form, is but a mass of habits, practical, emotional, and intellectual, systematically organized for our weal or woe, and bearing us irresistibly toward our destiny, whatever the latter may be.

~ William James
<u>Talks to Teachers</u>, Harvard, 1892

WHY DO HABITS EXIST?

That question apparently has never been asked, or maybe just hasn't been asked enough. If you Google "Why do humans exist?" you will at least get some search results that will link you to some interesting speculations, but what about the question, "Why do habits exist?"

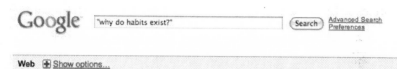

A Google search is by no means the definitive research tool, but for purposes of illustration and the pulse of pop culture, Google is a solid indicator of what is on the minds of the two billion people online. No one appears to have asked, or found the answer to, the question, "Why do habits exist?"[3]

You might think this is a nonsensical, unanswerable question, much like, "Why do people exist?" However, at

---

[3] Since this book was originally published, the search results have changed. I wrote a post about this (toward end): http://www.thehabitfactor.com/2012/11/beyond-the-power-of-habit-the-habit-factor-how-to-break-bad-habits-build-good-habits-part-one-get-unstuck-and-more/

last count there were 292,000 results matching that exact query on Google.

Perhaps it's better to try and understand, "What purpose do habits serve?" The theory goes that since they exist, chances are good they serve some purpose. *Correct?*

VICE OR VIRTUE?

Before we can go any further, we ought to play a quick word-association game. I'll give you the word and you say the first thing that pops into your head. Ready? "Habit."

Now please take a moment to look away or put the book down and say a word or two that comes to mind right away.

Did you say "smoking" or "swearing" or "drinking" or "TV" or "get elbows off the table," or my personal favorite, "chewing with your mouth open"?

On the other hand, what are the chances you said "wake up early," "drinking lots of water," "calling my friends," "kissing my wife/husband/significant other first thing every morning," "reading to my kids at night," "eating an apple a day," "working out every other day," or "jogging three times a week"?

To witness this "game" in action, please check the hyperlink below where I query a few kids outside a stadium just before a soccer game. While this video is pretty funny—it only underscores the importance of educating our future generations about habit and its significance to one's overall character, effectiveness, goal achievement and ultimate success[4].

This word-association game is one I use with people all the time, whether the word is habit or something else. Since everyone views the world differently, our best chance to see eye to eye is to first understand the other's perspective.

For instance, I had a conversation with a very smart software engineer who works at Qualcomm. He wanted to understand The Habit Factor better, so I explained (surface-level) briefly, "The Habit Factor helps people to create and track habits that assist them in achieving their goals."

He then did something amusing – that head-tilt thing my dog does when she's trying to process language. So, as engineer-guy digested that sentence for himself (remember, he's a very bright programmer), he then replied with a slight twinkle in his eye, "You know what? I just thought about that … anyone who achieves a goal must have created some really positive habits to achieve that goal."

BINGO!

This sort of exchange has continued for the last few years. It doesn't seem to matter with whom I speak – doctors, lawyers, entrepreneurs, even trainers and coaches – the light goes on in the same manner, and there's a certain shift in understanding. Even as I write this, what can be found about habits and goals and their unique relationship is confined to a handful of research papers, and those that

---

[4] https://www.youtube.com/watch?v=T5KpylqA9MU

actually do investigate the "Habit – Goal Interface" do so largely from the position of goals "guiding the formation of habit associations."

For example, as of this writing, a current Wikipedia article on "Habit (psychology)," where the habit goal interface is elaborated upon, includes the following explanation, "Goals guide habits most fundamentally by providing the initial outcome-oriented impetus for response repetition. In this sense, habits often are a vestige of past goal pursuit."[5] Really? Goals achieved equals habits created?

Where do we find anyone telling us the inverse of that statement – that carefully crafted habits identified to support a goal will invariably make the achievement of that goal a reality far more quickly? To say that a "habit is a vestige of a past goal pursuit" is almost like saying a best-selling book will make a well-written book. Sounds a little (or a lot) backwards to me.

The fact is, as a society we're still stuck at the same awareness level of our habits as we were when William James lectured about the very topic at Harvard in the late 1800s, and he was only lecturing in terms of vices and virtues (not goal achievement)! It is that fundamental awareness that was absent then and remains missing for most people, even today. Bear in mind his final sentence:

---

[5] Wikipedia article has been edited; as of this writing the most recent update is Nov. 15, 2014. Yet it is still presented from a context of habit as a negative/not serving goals. "When the habit prevails over the conscious goal, a capture error has taken place." What does that mean?

"All our life, so far as it has definite form, is but a mass of habits, practical, emotional, and intellectual, systematically organized for our weal or woe, and bearing us irresistibly toward our destiny, whatever the latter may be."

So, back to you. This word-association game is just a simple and straightforward litmus test to gauge how you regard and value the concept of habit right now: Does it relate to vice, virtue, or both?

If you associate habits with vices first, you are not alone. In fact, that is the common association (or mis-association) by the vast majority of people and is a problem for us all, collectively, as a society[6].

So, as we move forward, the first request is that you shift this fundamental association right away, as in now (please). In other words, habit must and will mean something radically different to you by the time you've completed this book. And, if that isn't the case, at the very least I'm hopeful we'll have presented new theories about habit that will aid you in applying an enhanced awareness to help you excel beyond your previous bounds.

---

[6] Informal surveys reveal nearly eight out of 10 people associate vices (negative connotations) *first* when considering the word habit. Now, consider the following New York Times article and its title, *"Warning: Habits May Be Good for You,"* July 13, 2008, and you can clearly see how pervasive these negative associations are throughout our culture and the media.

NEUTRALITY RULES

Now that I've got you to associate habits with virtues – positive traits, actions and characteristics – the truth is, habit is entirely impartial. Habit wields its force for either good or evil, and with little regard to any particular outcome.

Habit cares not where you are or who you are. Habit lives in the now and is always "on," so to speak, in recording mode. HABIT IS LANGUAGE. It's the language of action, and it communicates our intentions to the creative force (more on this a little later). This "recording" applies to learning and reminds me of the Socratic statement, "Learning is remembering," or perhaps even better, the Chinese proverb, "Tell me and I'll forget; show me and I may remember; involve me and I will understand."

Have you ever heard the axiom, "Guns don't kill people – people kill people"? The concept, of course, is that guns aren't bad and they aren't good either; as a neutral device, weapon or tool, they have saved lives as well as ended lives. Similarly, with habit, you have the ability to craft habits at will that can harm you or help you. Indeed, you have been handed a metaphorical gun to use for your "woe or weal."

"NO! YOU DON'T UNDERSTAND!" (RESPECTFULLY)

One of my best friends growing up was a guy named Brenny. Besides being a great friend, skier and all-around solid athlete, he had a very interesting habit when telling a story. Whether it was about skiing or surfing, he had to make certain that he added impact to his message – to convey, for example, just how gnarly the wave or the slope was. He would always grab the person he was talking to by both shoulders, shake them back and forth, and shout, "No! You don't understand!" Pretty endearing, actually.

Even as you stood there nodding your head in total agreement and fully comprehending what he was saying, he wanted to punctuate the message with a good shoulder shake. He was questioning your ability to grasp the significance of his message.

So, I find myself in similar situations these days when I try to emphasize the importance of habit in talks. Unfortunately, I can't pull off what Brenny got away with 20 years ago. However, having said that, I would like to respectfully grab both of your shoulders right now, give them a good shake, and yell (again, respectfully) as it relates to habit, "No! You don't understand!"

The Habit Factor can be of little value to you until you shift your perspective of habit, since how you view habit determines how much attention you give it, and how much attention you give it determines how you craft and guide your habits. A virtue is crafted through patient and diligent repetitive action (habit). And, favorable habits are crafted initially only through awareness. If you currently side with the majority of people who associate habit only with vice, as William James pointed out, now is the time for you to redefine what habit means.

Regrettably, both understanding and awareness of the significance of habit (itself), for the most part, doesn't seem to exist in our society – not from a standpoint of positivism. Some of you may disagree; rightly pointing out that popular self-help literature is littered with "habit"-related courses, books, etc. Even one of the most popular blogs on the Internet is entitled ZenHabits.

Well, yes and no. Yes, this type of literature emphasizes positive habits, and that is terrific. But, in seemingly all cases there is an associated list, number or recommended order of habits, where the emphasis is always on a specific habit or list. The fallacy in proceeding so narrowly and focusing only on a set of habits or a particular list is that circumstances and times change, but the principle force of habit does not. So, it seems to make little sense to exemplify and concentrate our efforts around a particular set of habits before we've attained a new, enlightened understanding of habit *itself*. Exactly when in our lives are we are taught about HABIT as the sole subject matter – as the core subject?

By redirecting our focus from a set of habits to HABIT itself as the subject matter, and focusing very deeply upon it, much like a diamond merchant might investigate his gem, we discover many new and unrealized dimensions of habit: biological, physiological, ecological, psychological, spiritual, environmental and behavioral, and even how they are ultimately interconnected. By studying habit this deeply, habit shifts from a passive afterthought to a recognized principle, a guiding force within our natural lives. In fact, habit is so powerful it connects our human nature to the supernatural. Yes, habit is the connecting link.

So it turns out my initial question of "Why do habits exist?" might be better asked: How could they NOT exist? That is, our human makeup (our CHARACTER-istics) must resemble the environment from which it came. And, whether you believe in God or not, know this: You were, in fact, created – that is, either through natural selection, evolution or some other process. You are a CREATURE. Carl Sagan, the famous astronomer and astrophysicist, once said, "If you want to create an apple pie from scratch, you first have to create the universe." Consider that statement for a minute. So why aren't most people attuned to the fact that our behavior patterns – our habits – ultimately must have the same sort of natural, powerful gravitational force as that in nature and of our universe?

A significant key to all achievement, then, is getting ourselves into the right orbit, that is, perfect harmony between our repetitive thoughts (habits), our desires and our daily actions (habits). Orison Swett Marden brilliantly stated, "Harmony is the key to all effectiveness." And so it is: Once you can integrate the habit of awareness into your daily behaviors, you can alter, redirect, and even substitute your reactions and behaviors at will to ensure they will serve your desired outcome.

Once this happens, major transformation is assured. Consider what changes you could make now and what would happen if you redefined your existing habits, beginning from such awareness?

GET STARTED!

So what keeps people from going after their goals and ideals? Well, that's an interesting question because the answer tends to reside in the very same place that habits reside: the subconscious. Typically, the inability to take that crucial first step involves a subconscious association with a future challenge, or possibly even pain.

Another reason people don't begin (start in pursuit of a goal) is they *believe* the process is ultimately just too overwhelming to undertake, no matter what it is; they are caught up in the idea that significant, large or massive actions are required to achieve their goals. However, upon further analysis, it's actually the exact opposite: A multitude of small, repeated actions over time can allow anyone to achieve their goal. Never forget Lao Tzu's classic quote, "The longest journey begins with a single step." In scientific terms this is simply called iteration – a process in which repetition of a sequence of operations yields results successively closer to a desired outcome.

Recall that upon setting foot on the moon, Neil Armstrong made his historic and uncannily perceptive declaration, "That's one *small* step for man; one giant leap for mankind." Notice he didn't put his foot down and declare, "That's one massive step for me!" He flawlessly acknowledged his "one small step" made possible by thousands of individuals who worked for nearly a decade coordinating millions of prior small actions.

In today's world, perhaps nobody represents the power of iteration better than Roz Savage, a remarkable woman and inspiration (note Foreword) who illustrates Lao Tzu's point magnificently. In 2010 she became the first woman to row solo across the Pacific Ocean. Coupled with her solo row across the Atlantic in 2005-2006, she has now rowed more than 11,000 miles, taken 3.5 million oar strokes, and spent cumulatively nearly a year of her life at sea in a 23-foot rowboat. Trust me when I tell you that Roz fully grasps the concept of iteration and the power of small, repeated actions over time. I love her quote, "Every action counts." That message is profound! (She also has her own corollary to the Nike slogan, but you'll have to watch one of her videos to find it. Here's a hint, though: The acronym is JFDI.)

Another common mistake when it comes to achievement and goal setting seems to be our collective focus upon only a particular methodology or set of actions (habits) – some magic formula or solution du jour. However, when it comes to achievement, this would be like studying only the various points of sail, but never learning about the principles of the wind. To be a master sailor, it's important to understand the principles of wind – its nature (origins), related factors (weather, land masses, ocean patterns and tides), even how to best locate and harness its power for your particular purpose and unique destination. A master sailor can literally see the wind and even anticipate its change of direction.

As a creator, we can learn from such a perspective – not by narrowing our focus but by broadening our awareness. It's never been solely about a particular set of habits or methods since times change and new circumstances arise. Consider that every few years there is a new and trendier method for getting things done. Some prefer the FranklinCovey Day Planner method and some David Allen's GTD, and for others, perhaps another method entirely. This isn't to suggest these tools and practices aren't helpful, since they have proven to be very useful. However, the real magic lies in the complete appreciation, comprehension and application of the hidden force that empowers each and every system, and that is habit.

So, for those of you who feel "stuck"– and to reaffirm that it is iteration and not some sort of enormous action that is required to help you accomplish your goal – here's a simple reminder acronym: START (Simple Today Actions Repeated & Tracked). Focus your energies on getting started, today (*now*).

Your goal may not be to row across an ocean, but once you have identified your personal goal, consider even the simplest, tiny action that you could take today. Identify ahead of time just how many days a week you want to repeat these actions. Then continually TRACK them. **We will go into far greater detail about habit alignment and the habit-tracking process in the Application section.** For now, however, it is important for you to redefine and understand what it is going to take for you to achieve your goals, and that is small actions (behaviors) repeated (compounded) over time. In fact, how you got where you are right now is nothing other than a compilation of small actions over time. Nobody ever got rich or fat overnight! **Small actions compounded (*over time*) reveal massive results (*positive or negative*)!**

Jiddu Krishnamurti, the great Indian philosopher, once said, "To go far you must begin near, and the nearest step is the most important one." This is clearly what Roz and any great achiever knows. (Remember, there are no secrets!) There was no single, massive oar stroke that propelled Roz across the Pacific. While she did have a huge goal and vision, she kept her energies and attention focused on the near – the nearest step, or in her case, stroke.

So here is the fascinating part: Once you start your journey of small, repeated actions, it is as though each action has its own Newtonian-like gravitational force. Each subsequent time you perform the action, the resistance is slowly chipped away until finally it's completely gone! In fact, the force that was resisting your initial exertions ultimately does a sort of reverse polarity and becomes a pulling force. Runners find that after they've developed the habit of running, stopping would be as hard as starting used to be. Now that is real momentum!

Indeed, once something has become a positive, consciously crafted habit, it can be the most remarkable gem, an action that performs itself – and here's the best part – on autopilot, with the same natural ease and effortlessness that moves an entire planet rotating around the sun!

Simply put: Your first responsibility is to get into the habit of constantly refining your habits of thought and action. Consciously craft and practice new dynamics in your daily activities, starting with both thought and action. Recognize that while it may seem that way, there are no big, singular actions that ever stand alone to change your life. Any such moment is part of a long chain of prior moments and actions.

It's the smallest of actions (compounded via repetition) over time that yields the largest rewards. This comes only through patience, diligence and perseverance. Lao Tzu's realizations are paramount here: By managing the easy, you can anticipate the difficult, and a journey of a thousand miles begins with a single step.

As a society, it seems we've now forged a habit of seeking "quick-fix" type solutions to solve our major societal issues, whether it's our education system, the health care system, our economy or even the environment. This is peculiar because we must recognize that it wasn't one drastic action that turned each of these areas upside down. And, we certainly should recognize that none of these problems will be corrected overnight via some silver bullet, such as legislation or financial aid. In fact, it was years (in some cases hundreds of years) of compounded neglect and misdirected action that damaged or broke each. So it stands to reason that the only path to resolution must be the inverse of the path of destruction: simple, positive, small, individual actions, performed daily.

HABITS TAKE 2, OR NAPOLEON HILL 101

Napoleon Hill was originally a newspaper writer (in the early 1900s) and was selected by Andrew Carnegie, the world's first billionaire, to write a book about the principles for personal achievement, encapsulating the "laws" for success in what Hill would later label his "Philosophy of Achievement." Carnegie wanted to ensure that his lifetime of lessons and "secrets" for achievement would not go untold. He felt an obligation to share the many lessons he believed were responsible for the billions of dollars he amassed and the enriched life he enjoyed.

Napoleon agreed to take on Carnegie's project and reportedly dedicated 20 years to the effort. The result would become one of the all-time best-selling books, *Think and Grow Rich*. Part of his study included unique access to many of the most successful men of the time, including Charles M. Schwab, Theodore Roosevelt, John D. Rockefeller, Thomas Edison and Henry Ford, to name a few.

Even today, *Think and Grow Rich* continues to be a best seller and, more importantly, is credited by many of today's most successful people and top personal development coaches and authors, such as Brian Tracy, John C. Maxwell, Jack Canfield and others, as one of the preeminent books on personal achievement.

Following the book's release, Napoleon toured the country giving inspirational speeches. And while Napoleon inspired millions of people with his best-selling book and helped to create many success stories, he remained somewhat confounded by the large number of people who approached him or wrote him letters to tell him, "The book didn't work." They didn't make a million dollars. They, in fact, did not become rich.

Napoleon was frustrated by such criticism, and in his own words recognized "something was missing." He said that he meditated on the "missing link" for years and ultimately discovered what he believed was the answer. He recompiled his formula for achievement, taking all the original 16 principles and adding one final, missing ingredient. He labeled this, "The Law of Cosmic Habit Force."

You see, ultimately he realized that the reason some people didn't achieve their desired results was that they didn't consistently take action. He noted that in each case he studied, while the students might be applying each principle at one time or another, there was randomness. There was no deliberate and routine execution of these principles. In short, the students failed to create habits of the essential 16[7] principles of thought and action.

Ultimately, everyone defines success differently, if they define it at all (which is curious, since certainly everyone seems to want it). It is simply and profoundly important for everyone to recognize that there is a consistent ingredient

---

[7] Hill notes that the 17th principle is the "Law of Cosmic Habit Force" in The Science of Personal Achievement by Nightingale Conant, which ties together the other 16 principles. Correction: prior edition noted 15 vs. 16.

that can be traced throughout history, identified in all success and achievement small and large – a trait so obvious, so observable it's become obfuscated. Tragically, somehow, it's become the real secret in personal development.

You see, even The Secret (the popular book and self-help movement advocating the "Law of Attraction") itself cannot work without the established power of habit – without The Habit Factor. Just the other day, one of The Secret's original contributors posted a YouTube video about the Law of Attraction and "why the Law of Attraction does not work properly or positively for like 99 percent of the population." He goes on to say, "I actually think it might be 99.9 percent." Care to guess what the answer is?

Much like success, each of us tends to define happiness a little differently, or at least what makes us happy. And therein lays one of the first mistakes: the quality of the question being asked. In this case, it shouldn't be "*what* makes us happy," but an acknowledgement that for enduring happiness, the responsibility falls *within*.

From my experience, the happiest people I've ever met are the most responsible people – that is, they take ownership of their circumstances and their condition. Responsibility is an essential attribute of happiness; it's the core foundation of happiness. This is what Buddha meant when he said, "There is no way to happiness – happiness is the way."

So, a core precept of The Habit Factor is to take responsibility, to take control and consciously craft your thoughts (beliefs) actions and behaviors into favorable and constructive habits, habits that align with your goals to help you create your ideal future – your success.

When you craft constructive habits, you serve yourself, your community and ultimately the planet. Responsibility and ownership ultimately fall upon the individual. Hence, the best way to improve the world can only be to improve yourself.

The Habit Factor is part research, part theory and part application, and if there is a single mission of this book, it's to radically redefine human awareness or, more specifically, *your* understanding and awareness of habit. The idea is to alter and shift your awareness so dramatically that it moves habit from the background as a passing, passive afterthought and drives it so far forward mentally that it becomes a primary filter for processing and designing your life.

This requires a paradigm shift where everything from goals to the lifestyle you wish to create is first routed through a habit *gateway* – an awareness of simple questions processed through the following reflective statement: "What habits must I have to help me get there?" This is much like a sailor might ask, "What point of sail must I take to achieve my destination?" It is this questioning and reasoning with respect and appreciation for the laws of the wind that helps a captain realize his destination more quickly and easily.

Similarly, there is nothing of greater impact to our "realities" than our subconscious – the incredible power of the subconscious can be likened to the power of the wind. By working with this force and *aligning your intentions and habits with it*, you too will reach your desired destination more quickly and easily, every time. In fact, know this: It's impossible to reach your destination when you are out of alignment with the wind.

Thus, we understand why experience remains the best teacher. It's virtually impossible for a child to absorb the significance of habit until there have been years of experience upon which to reflect, and for her to notice the profound impact habit has played upon her life to present her with her current situation. This may explain why you tend to see so many profound quotes about habit not from young scholars but from the aged, the wise men and women who are able to reflect back over a lifetime of habits to see those traits and trials that brought their arrival.

Returning to the sailing metaphor, as soon as the skill of sailing "clicked" and I understood the nuances of the wind in addition to the points of sail, not only was sailing much easier and more fun, but I sailed from a new perspective (in alignment with the laws of the wind). I could easily pick up the subtle cues about how tight to have each sail for maximum "trim," or what might be the quickest way to get to any destination. I was able to read the waters ahead, notice any wind changes and actually identify where the wind would be the strongest. I could effectively anticipate my next maneuvers and actions.

Yes, the wind literally took me (once I understood its principles) wherever I chose to go. I could simply harness this gift – this magical force – and the same is true with habit. The ability to harness the most powerful force in a human's arsenal – the subconscious – is rooted not through hypnosis but in habit. Perform an action repeatedly, and the body and mind communicate to the creative force that this is indeed the direction you wish to go. You've raised the sails of your subconscious, and now they will continue to work in your favor even when you are not consciously performing your actions.

We live in an enigmatic and paradoxical world, one where Lao Tzu announced nearly 3,000 years ago, "The softest things in the world overcome the hardest." Yet, we find ourselves in a relentless search for a secret that will improve our lives and reshape our destiny. The irony, of course, is that if we are fortunate, we recognize before it's too late that what we've sought has been literally within.

Indeed, we are in control. By identifying, modifying and creating the proper habits (including our thoughts), we reshape our destiny.

Note: The final pages of each section will outline some *precepts* (rules and principles for action) shared within the section. After the ideas are summarized in outline form, there are a few exercises to help underscore the messages. As you pursue your own goals you may find it handy to revisit the precept summaries as a quick reference.[8]

---

[8] For Audiobook or ebook readers who want these final section precepts and actions worksheets, please visit: http://thehabitfactor.com/templates.

Introduction Precepts
(Ideas and Principles for Action)
<u>Ideas</u>

- Individually and collectively, it's important to redefine our common and typically negative associations of habit.
- The only way to craft a virtue is via habit. Therefore we should regard habit in a positive context.
- The "Habit-Goal" relationship has been overlooked for far too long and is misunderstood.
- Establishing proper, related habits for any goal helps one achieve their goal much more quickly and easily.
- Habit is neutral and either serves you or works against you.
- Habit is multidimensional and it intersects our lives on all levels: astronomy, biology, psychology, sociology, ecology, etc.
- Habit is the connecting device that bridges the conscious mind to the subconscious and to Infinite Intelligence.
- Habit is a language of creation and achievement.
- As the universe is governed by certain laws, so too are our personal characteristics. Consider rhythm and pattern, repeated behavior.
- The most important part of all achievement is to get *started*, to break the inertia and get moving. Habit makes our efforts easier – over time.
- It is iteration, not huge action, which enables achievement.
- There are no secrets to achievement and success.
- Habit is a force that can be likened to the wind. As a skilled sailor works within the principles of the wind to arrive at his destination, you too must work with the principle force of Habit.

Actions!

∞ List 1 *new* Habit in each category that, if you developed it, would dramatically alter your results. For instance, Finance habit, "Saving \$10/day." Health habit, "Drink 6 glasses of water a day."
Circle the one you want to focus on developing first!

∞ List your best habit for each category: Mind, Body (Health), Social, Spiritual, Professional, Family, Financial
Mind: _____   Professional: _____
Body: _____   Family: _____
Social: _____   Financial: _____
Spiritual: _____

∞ List your single worst habit for each of the above categories.
Circle the one you want to correct first!
Mind: _____   Professional: _____
Body: _____   Family: _____
Social: _____   Financial: _____
Spiritual: _____

∞ What is habit? Write out your new association.

HABITS: THE SCIENTIFIC

Habit

- a behavior pattern acquired through frequent repetition, regularly followed until it becomes almost involuntary: *the habit of looking both ways before crossing the street.*

- a dominant or regular disposition or tendency; prevailing character or quality: *a habit of looking at the bright side of things.*

The American Heritage Dictionary
of the English Language, Fourth Edition

"Habit is stronger than reason."
~George Santayana

CREATURES OF HABIT

Humans are, *by nature*, creatures of habit. It's widely reported that up to 95 percent of our thoughts and 45 percent of our behaviors are based on habit. If you think about it, most of our daily activities are a product of habit: when and how we get up in the morning, the way we shower, brush our teeth, get dressed, read the paper, eat, drive to work ... the course of each day is directed by literally hundreds of our habits.

The reality is, the habits we possess – or fail to possess – wield significant influence over us and go far deeper than just our daily routines. Our habits affect every aspect of our lives and have a ripple effect that impacts not just us but our friends and family. *Ultimately, habits shape our destiny.*

In fact, your character (or the current condition of your character) is essentially defined by how you are regarded by your friends and family and is nothing other than their assessment and interpretation of your habits of both thought and action. Thus, the definition and Latin root of the word "habit" is most fascinating: "condition or character." Your current condition and your character are the sum of your habits to this moment.

This notion that our habits fashion and dictate our character is truly old school. Aristotle, in 350 B.C., proclaimed: "It is the habit of just and temperate actions that produces virtue." Cicero proclaimed, "Habit is, as it were, a second nature." During the past century, numerous researchers and theorists have put forth many arguments on how human lives are shaped by the realm of habit. Beyond this observation, however, scholarly conceptualization of habit is still widely divergent, ranging from the scientific (habit as neural networks or conditioned responses) to the esoteric (habit as custom, ritual, rite or ceremony).

WELCOME TO YOUR BRAIN (WHICH IS NOT YOUR MIND)

One of the most common misnomers tends to be the casual interchange between two words that are in actuality rather different. It seems even the most noted scholars and doctors casually interchange the words *mind* and *brain* (sometimes even in the same sentence) as though they were the same thing. I noticed this when watching a special on brain plasticity on television. It was interesting that the feature was focused upon the brain, yet the term "mind" was so often interchanged. Know this: The mind is not the brain. The theory here, as it relates to understanding the component parts of achievement, presupposes your brain is only *part* of your mind.

The brain is an organ. It's quantifiable, measurable and certainly available to current methods of scientific study. The mind, on the other hand, takes on a mystical and spiritual quality. You can point to your brain, but I've never seen a doctor show me where the mind is. Neurosurgeons can work on and study the brain and prescribe medications for the brain, but the mind is a whole different, transcendent vehicle. We'll revisit this subject a little later in the Esoteric section. For now, though, let's focus on what science can literally put its fingers on, and that is your brain.

The limbic system, often alluded to as the "emotional brain," is part of our forebrain that is buried within the cerebrum. The term "limbic" was formally introduced by Dr. Paul MacLean in 1952 and comes from the Latin *limbus*, loosely translating as "border." Structures of the limbic system include the amygdala, basal ganglia, hippocampus, hypothalamus, olfactory cortex and thalamus.

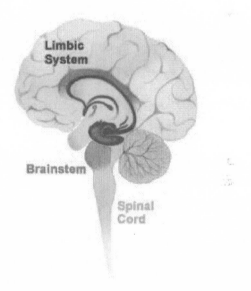

The limbic system is also tightly connected to the prefrontal cortex. In the past, this connection was sometimes surgically severed to cure severe emotional disorders, a psychosurgery procedure called a prefrontal lobotomy. Patients who underwent this procedure often became passive and lacked all motivation after the operation.

The limbic system supports a wide variety of functions involving emotion, behavior and long-term memory, all of which directly impact the habits we create. Think back to when you first learned to drive a car. Every single aspect of the process demanded your complete concentration. Chances are good you were carefully engaged as you squeezed the steering wheel tightly with both hands (10 and two o'clock positions) and leaned forward, worried that at any moment you might run someone over or make some other awful mistake.

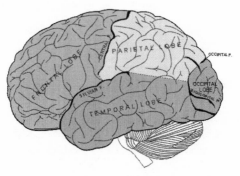

During that first driving experience, your intense focus engaged your conscious "executive brain" (the frontal lobe), while your "habitual brain" (subconscious) was just along for the ride (so to speak). However, rest assured, your limbic structures weren't just freeloading – they were in record mode.

As time progressed, you went from being a nervous wreck behind the steering wheel to becoming rather capable, with few worries. Soon, you were able to stop thinking cognitively about all things driving related. In fact, over time, your brain learned to pass along all the driving instructions to the habitual part of your brain, allowing for the executive, conscious brain to focus on other items of importance.

This is precisely why, for so many people, time spent in their cars is often creative or even relaxing, since they can just cruise and let their minds wander. The wonderful lady who cuts my hair just told me last week how much she enjoys her one-hour-plus commute. "I can just unwind ... it's a perfect way to relax after a stressful day." My guess is if you should happen to be driving on a familiar road, you may not even think twice about how to navigate from one point to the next; everything about the drive is managed by the habitual brain. However, if you were to encounter an accident or happen upon a detour then, suddenly, your intellectual brain would kick in.

Our limbic structures are designed for routine tasks, not new challenges. When confronted with an unexpected development in a typically habitual situation, our limbic structures redirect the assignment to the executive brain. This helps to illustrate an important difference between the two mechanisms of the brain. The limbic system processes routine tasks quickly, without conscious thought, and the executive brain handles the challenges of new tasks.

OF MICE AND MEN

Dr. Ann Graybiel, a professor of neurophysiology at MIT, decided to study a particular area of the limbic system: the basal ganglia. The basal ganglia is a deep, primordial region of the brain that controls our movement and cognition, as well as our ability to absorb habits. Disorders in this area are connected to Parkinson's and Huntington's diseases, as well as neuropsychiatric disorders such as Tourette's syndrome, obsessive-compulsive disorder, depression and addiction.

In one study, Dr. Graybiel tracked the activity of the brains of some mice through implanted electrodes, so she could identify when neurons were firing. The rodents' task was to navigate a maze. Each time a mouse attempted the maze the first time, the basal ganglia was constantly firing, but as the mouse began to master the maze, the basal ganglia became far less active.

This discovery revealed our basal ganglia to be a sort of recording device, memorizing segments of repeated behaviors that might later enable us to operate on autopilot. When you climb into your car, ready for your drive home, you've entered a habitat that is all too familiar. Such comfort provides the necessary cues your basal ganglia needs to switch to autopilot. Then, before you know it, you're parking your car. I can recall leaving the office one night after a challenging day, my head spinning with solutions, strategies and possible outcomes. The next thing I knew, I found myself parking my car in my garage. I literally said aloud, "Did I just drive home?"

LEARNING SYSTEMS

Scientists posit that there are two chief systems of learning: cognitive and habit. The cognitive component relies on the prefrontal cortex, while the habit module relies on the dorsal striatum, a major input station of the basal ganglia system. Anatomically, the striatum is part of an area of the brain known as the caudate.

The brain has two major structural and functional components: the thinking brain (neocortex) and the feeling/emotional brain (limbic cortex). These two areas are in constant communication, as the neocortex attempts to modulate the powerful urges coming from the limbic brain. The limbic structures, such as the amygdala and hippocampus (shown below), are buried deep within the neocortex. It's theorized that as the brain developed, the neocortical areas grew on top of the limbic areas.

Thus, the limbic areas are often labeled the "old brain" and the neocortical areas the "new brain." In terms of strategy and decision-making, the neocortical areas remain slow and cognitive; in other words, they deliberate. The limbic areas are quick, often non-rational, and are not self-aware; in other words, they remain subject to influence.

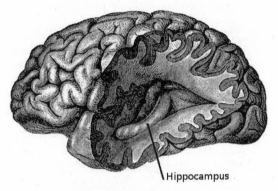

Hippocampus

There is an interesting relationship at play as these two areas of the brain either lead to psychological agreement or conflict. These conditions are either labeled dissonance (incongruous) or consonance (harmony). (Note: Please remember consonance and harmony later when we investigate the importance of harmonic energies and achievement.)

By understanding our brain makeup, we can appreciate how the brain communicates to itself via the neurons and the synaptic connections that travel from one brain region to another. The more frequent the connections, the greater the likelihood the pathway becomes entrenched and a connection is created to the limbic structure.

You may recall just how difficult the "simple" act of tying your shoelaces was as a kid. In fact, it might have taken you days to learn. You may have even cried from the frustration. Kids everywhere between 5-7 years old are terrified by the notion that they may be the only ones in their class who can't tie their shoes. Today, chances are good you perform this habit without any conscious thought. You don't even need to look down, and you're probably even thinking about something entirely unrelated to the task at hand. This is a fantastic example of your cognitive brain handing over the once complex but now routine task of shoelace tying to the limbic brain, where it is stored as habit.

TABULA RASA

Aristotle is thought to be the first to propose that the human intellect at first can be likened to a clean tablet on which nothing is written. He referred to this as *tabula rasa,* or "unscribed slate." The idea is each of us is born as an empty slate, and our experiences, authority figures and other influences begin to program us in our formative years. For instance, upon birth it was as though your brain's computer was empty. You didn't even have an operating system. But, with each and every new experience – each time a sense was triggered (energy), sight, taste, touch or smell – your brain's operating system began to be programmed by these new experiences.

Learning something and figuring it out for the first time involves the cognitive system, or the prefrontal cortex. But once that sequence becomes habit, the habit takes over. In habit mode, you just do it... because you've always just done it. Habits, then, should be viewed as stored solutions or even thought energy made efficient. Just be sure you are storing/memorizing the correct solutions.

The Drive Reduction theory offered by Clark L. Hull (between 1929 and 1952) was one of the most detailed and complex habit theories. The basic concept involved "habit strength," which depicts habits as stimulus-response connections strengthened by rewards, which develop as a function of practice. Hull wanted to understand all the variables that might affect behavior, such as original drive, incentives, inhibitors, and prior training (habit strength). As with other behavioral theories, reinforcement proved to be the leading factor affecting learning. This too dictated whether or not habits would in fact take root and become automatic.

In Hull's theory, need and drive play an important role in behavior and habit formation. For instance: A six-year-old girl is told that there is candy hidden under one of the books in a bookcase. She pulls out many books at first in a random manner, and then finally discovers the correct book (taking 210 seconds). Once again, more candy is hidden under the same book, and in her next search she is more direct and targeted, finding the candy in 86 seconds. By her ninth attempt, the subject finds the candy nearly immediately (in two seconds).

It was the girl's initial drive for the candy that produced her responses. By ultimately identifying the correct book, she was rewarded and would repeat this response. This repetition formed a habit. Finally, as the strength of the habit was increased, it ultimately became a *single* stimulus-response connection (nearly instant!).

In 2009, *The Journal of Neuroscience* published a research study entitled "Stress Prompts Habit Behavior in Humans." There continues to be a lot of debate as to how well humans really operate in times of stress – some people think stress facilitates our abilities, while others believe stress brings out other less positive behaviors, but the question these researchers really had was whether or not stress directed people's reactions in comparing cognitive versus habit-related choices.

These researchers took a group of 80 college students, who rated orange juice and chocolate pudding as being equally valuable to them. They brought the students into a room and provided as many oranges or as much chocolate pudding as they could eat until they were satiated. This was supposed to make the orange or the pudding similar to a habit – it was something they got all the time.

They then separated the group; half under a non-stressful condition and the other half exposed to a stressful condition. To stress the second group of students, they were instructed to hold their hand in ice water until their heart rate and blood pressure went up, and they were producing increased levels of the stress hormone cortisol.

All the students were then brought into a room where they were given a choice of oranges or chocolate pudding. In the case of the non-stressed group of students, they shied away from what they were already heavily exposed to. So, for instance, if they had been eating chocolate pudding, they preferred orange juice instead.

However, when it came to the stressed group, something entirely different took place. Even though they had already eaten either chocolate pudding or oranges until they were sated, due to the stress, they selected their habit choice. They might have been tired of pudding, but stress seemed to make the choice easier, even when they weren't realizing any further enjoyment from it. *They continued choosing the same thing out of habit.* When asked afterward, the stressed students even had a hard time remembering their choices, since they were acting out of habit without any regard to what the actions or consequences meant.

HABITAT

Habitat might be defined as "the area or natural environment in which an organism or population normally lives." So, is it any wonder why our *environment* plays such a vital role in our habit development, retention and – when it comes time to break them – dissolution?

Every day at 11:15 a.m., people from within our office complex file outside to kill themselves. They gather slowly, and one by one they light up their cigarettes. On some level, I'm nearly positive they recognize this habit is killing them; however, it's their *environment* and *routine* that has become so familiar, providing so much reassurance that somehow it makes this form of slow suicide not only bearable, but apparently enjoyable.

Typically, behind any habit you will find a family of other habits or "cues" (sometimes called triggers) involved in its formation. And tragically, in the case of our office complex, should any one of those individuals ever decide they want to quit smoking, they have a significant uphill battle ahead of them regardless of what method or product they elect to use to quit their smoking habit. Because, as I'm sure you recognize, you can't spell habitat without spelling habit, and any successful habit-cessation strategy must first take into account the habitat and all the related cues.

It is troubling to discover a smoker still won't quit even after learning that smoking is a leading cause of death, or that a person who is obese lacks drive or motivation to change even after learning about the lethal ailments that loom. Researchers like Dr. Wendy Wood, formerly of Duke University, and Dr. Brian Wansink, formerly of Cornell University, studied related habit and environmental cues, for example, how often smokers might quit if they are on vacation, and how much people might eat if their plates and servings are deceptively altered.[ii]

Dr. Wansink decided to experiment with a bowl of tomato soup that was discreetly attached to a tube that continuously pumped more soup into the bowl. Although the diners ended up eating nearly twice their usual amount, interestingly, they didn't report feeling any more full.

Dr. Wood examined the exercise habits of student athletes who transferred from one college to another. If the new school had an outdoor track similar to the old school, the students continued to run regularly. However, if the tracks were too dissimilar (indoor vs. outdoor), the training habit, on average, began to taper off. Other experiments demonstrate that smokers are *more than twice as successful at quitting if they initiate their cessation while on a vacation.*

These and other studies verify what we may already intuit: Much of our daily behaviors are habitual, performed without cognitive thought and usually related to a series of subtle cues. These cues tend to fall into four general categories: a specific location or time of day, a series of actions, the company of specific people or particular moods.

Often habits and addictions coexist, but it's important to distinguish the two. Habit is synonymous with routine, tendency and inclination, whereas addiction is a fixation, chemical dependency or even an obsession. For example, when trying to change the habit of smoking, there is both a habit and an addiction involved. People who smoke have varying degrees of habit and addiction, but it's important to realize that *addiction* is the chemical dependency to the nicotine; the rest is habit.

This brings to the fore the idea of positive versus negative reinforcement. Alcohol is a great example: The "rewarding" properties at first entice people to come back for more. However, after too much consumption, the negative properties, such as getting sick or experiencing hangovers, begin to associate themselves. As the drinker consumes more alcohol, the negative associations typically override the positive ones, helping most people to moderate their consumption.

It is important to note that the same environmental triggers that initiate habituated responses also facilitate the development of new habits. One sure way to be more successful at cultivating habits is to involve the other senses.

An example for me was the necessity of developing a writing habit (to complete this book). This book was not going to get finished until I consciously crafted a habit of writing first thing in the morning. But the habit didn't come easy, and I found that I had to surround the habit with other related behaviors, including waking up at least an hour earlier, meditating for at least 12 minutes, and even stretching to help me to sit and write longer. The key associated behavior in this case was awakening earlier. I also prohibited myself from checking any e-mails until I was through writing. All these behaviors constituted my writing routine, and it's interesting to notice how many of these behaviors actually had nothing to do with the act of writing.

HABIT REVERSAL

Habit reversal, or behavior modification, has been practiced by psychotherapists, parents, teachers and even caretakers. The process involves the most basic methods to alter human behavior – a set of undesirable habits – through reward and punishment.

One of the simplest, yet most effective, methods of behavior modification is labeled the "ABC" approach, where observations are made on Antecedents, Behaviors and Consequences. In other words: (1) What took place directly *before* the behavior? This is an example of the cues or triggers as previously identified. (2) Identifying exactly what the behavior *looks* like, and (3) Capturing what takes place *after* the behavior.

Once enough observations are made, all data is scrutinized for *patterns*. If consistent patterns are identified with antecedents and/or consequences, then an intervention targets these behaviors in order to modify the behavior – increase or decrease its frequency.

Habit reversal is a multi-component treatment designed to address repetitive behaviors that may have any negative physical or social effects for the person. Pioneered by Nathan Azrin and others in 1973, habit reversal and its variations have been deemed effective for over 25 years in research across a spectrum of habits and related behaviors. Behavior modification procedures from the Applied Behavior Analysis tradition have proven useful in academics and even in the penal system.

As you've likely come to recognize, bad habits are extremely hard to eliminate because of their very powerful associations and neural wiring. A successful way to get rid of old habits is not to focus on eliminating the habit, but rather *replacing* it with a new, favorable habit. This is why the Dutch scholar Desiderius Erasmus as far back as the 15th century advised, "A nail is driven out by another nail. Habit is overcome by habit."

One of my very dear friends realized a few years ago that it was time to quit drinking, for good. Unfortunately, he had formed a habit of drinking 12 or more beers a day. On some level he recognized that the most effective way to stop drinking was *not* to stop drinking. That is, he kept the habit of drinking, but substituted non-alcoholic beer for the alcoholic beer. As it turns out, his habit of "cracking" a beer, holding a beer and even drinking and socializing were as much a part of his ritualistic consumption as the alcohol itself. So, rather than try to break all those related habits and the associated routines, Lance wisely opted for non-alcoholic beer. Now, whether it's at a golf outing or any other social event, Lance still enjoys all the related social and behavioral aspects of his prior drinking ritual, only now it's alcohol free.

Know that your best bet in removing any bad habit is to replace it with a favorable one. When you do this, you're following William James' profound advice of making your nervous system your ally instead of an enemy. In fact, James went even further to suggest that this technique (*aligning with your nervous system*) is an important educational tool. Educators everywhere, please consider the implications of his profound statement: *"The great thing in all of education is to make our nervous system our ally instead of our enemy."*

THE 21-DAY HABIT THEORY

Chances are fairly good that you've heard it takes 21 days to form a habit. This 21-day concept was originally introduced by Dr. Maxwell Maltz in his book titled *Psycho-Cybernetics*. Originally a plastic surgeon, Dr. Maltz noticed that after about 21 days amputees began to cease feeling phantom sensations in the amputated limb.

Dr. Maltz also noticed that many of his clients retained a poor self image even after plastic surgery that helped to improve their appearance. This provoked him to work with his clients' self image before surgery, and in many cases he tried to dissuade them altogether from surgery. He later discovered that he could help them improve their self-image without surgery, using a 21-day period to create a new image and mindset.

From further observations, Dr. Maltz found a pattern emerging: The human mind appeared to take almost exactly 21 days to adapt to a life change, whether it's a negative, such as the loss of a limb, job or a loved one; or a positive adjustment, such as entering into a new romantic relationship, or moving into a new home.

The theory behind this is that brain circuits generate neuroconnections and neuropathways only when they are fired upon for 21 days in a row. In a sense, Maltz was far ahead of his time. Today, neuroplasticity (which suggests the brain is malleable based upon experience throughout one's life) is a new and developing science, where formerly, theories suggested the brain was immutable after the developing stages of childhood. According to Maltz, 21 days (without missing a day) was the magic number to embed new habits.

The essence of Dr. Maltz's technique is to simply devote 15 minutes a day to the formation of any habit, and perform it faithfully for 21 days. By the fourth week, the new behavior should be so rooted that it will be harder *not* to engage in it than to continue doing it. This applies to any type of habit, whether it is a physical practice or a way of perceiving something, such as a self image.

Maltz's identification that it essentially takes 21 days to create a new habit is enlightening, but it is also important to note that 21 days is *not* a magic number. Not from my experience. I've noticed, both personally and with people I've worked with, that some habits take far longer to develop (three months or more). I've also noticed that habits can be developed with "gaps" – days of non-habit behavior. In fact, a key attribute in The Habit Factor's methodology is the ability to identify "target" days that, contrary to Maltz's theory, allow for habit formation without the successive-day requirement. Since some habits, such as jogging, aren't likely to be daily requirements, the most important factor in the formation of any habit is *consistency over time*. With The Habit Factor, this can be attained through refined "tracking periods" that will be elaborated upon in the Application section.

Science has proven that habits can help to keep us safe and make our life easier. When habit is engaged, we save precious energy as we accomplish worthwhile and practical tasks without conscious thought. In this regard, it's fairly easy to liken habit with a form of human auto-pilot.

However, the closer we can draw our investigation of habit to its essence (our essence) – that of our universal nature – the more fully we can appreciate and tap into this supernatural gift that facilitates achievement and creation. This gift is habit, and it's been bestowed upon everyone.

Yet, unfortunately, habit remains understood by few and *esteemed* by even fewer. This leads us conveniently into the realm of the mystical – the *esoteric* dominion of habit.

The Scientific, Precepts
(Ideas and Principles for Action)
Ideas

- The brain is not the mind. The brain is the organ. The mind is the metaphysical link connecting the subconscious to Infinite Intelligence.
- Habits reside in the emotional part of the brain, the limbic region, and this is where the subconscious mind resides.
- Limbic structures are designed to handle multiple tasks at once.
- The executive mind (prefrontal cortex) doesn't multitask well.
- The basil ganglia acts as a recording device.
- Learning systems: The brain has two major structural divisions: neocortex (thinking) and limbic cortex (feeling/emotional). Limbic is fast, less than rational and not self-aware.
- Habits should be viewed as stored solutions. Be sure you are storing the right information!
- Rewards increase habit strength, and stress drives behavior to default to old habits, favorable or unfavorable.
- Habitats (environments) provide related habit cues and associations.
- Changing environments helps to change habits.
- Four broad *cues* for habit associations are: specific location or time of day, prior series of actions, moods and company (specific people).
- Addiction is a chemical dependency; habit is not.
- Involving multiple senses helps to strengthen habit formation.
- Habits are strengthened by consistency *over time*, not necessarily consecutive days.

Actions!

∞ List one ritual that is part of your day and identify one habit that, if altered (replaced with a more constructive habit), will positively affect your results. Example: Noon/lunch – take time after lunch to rest 10 minutes, check e-mail, surf Web. New habit: "reading trade journal." No Web surfing until after lunch.

∞ Review your Morning, Noon and Night rituals; recount a set of habits around each. Example: Morning – out of bed by 6:30 a.m., meditate, stretch, drink water before coffee, eat apple.

∞ Identify ways you could alter or redefine a bad habit's environment and any associated habits/cues. List one or two cues. Identify a change or new environment.

∞ List one reward you might use to motivate yourself if you could establish a new habit. Note: In the Application section we'll review in detail how to create a new habit. For right now, it's just good to associate the successful creation of a habit to a reward that motivates you. Example: "No Web surfing before 6 p.m." for 60 days might yield a new iPad.

HABITS: THE ESOTERIC

Esoteric

Understood by or meant for only the
select few who have special
knowledge or interest; translated from
Greek, *esoterikos* – meaning,
"Belonging to an inner circle."

Originally of Pythagorean doctrines;
the division of teachings into exoteric
and esoteric originated with Aristotle.

-   Online Etymology Dictionary, © 2001

---

*"The last function of reason is to recognize
there are an infinity of things which surpass it."*
~Blaise Pascal

THE UNIVERSE AND COSMOS

"Ill habits gather by unseen degrees;
as brooks make rivers, rivers run to seas."
~ Ovid

Indeed! Habits straddle and encompass an esoteric border that connects the minute to the great, the micro to the macro. In so doing, habit links science to art by straddling a cryptic and often enigmatic sphere that exists within our minds. This is a connection to the super-conscious, to a macrocosm of our relative spheres of influence, both figurative and literal. Such natural, recurring motifs should be of little surprise since, upon further analysis, it's our behaviors (our habits) that represent a microcosm of the macro – the governing and unchanging natural laws of our universe.

The word "universe" translates directly from Latin and its literal meaning is "one turn," often interpreted as "one song." In a physical sense, the universe refers to all matter and energy, including the Earth, the galaxies and intergalactic space; it also refers to the Earth, including all created things – its inhabitants and humans.

In the opening two sentences from Sir Bertrand Russell's book *What I Believe* from 1925, the great philosopher and Nobel Prize winner writes, "Man is a part of Nature, not something contrasted with Nature. His thoughts and his bodily movements follow the same laws that describe the motions of the stars and atoms."

Regardless of how you look at the universe and even the word itself, this much is clear: All the cosmos, our entire universe, is undeniably one grand, magical and mysterious song. And, it's the universe's own nature to follow predetermined rhythms and patterns – nature's very own form of habit.

German mathematician and astronomer Johannes Kepler (1571–1630) discovered three laws of planetary motion to describe the movement of planets in the solar system: The orbit of a planet is an ellipse with the sun at its focus; planets travel equal areas in equal times; and the square of the period of an orbit is proportional to the cube of the average radius – in other words, the relationship between the planet's average radius and its orbital period always came up to the same number.

These laws permit the exact location of planets and stars today to be precisely predicted centuries ago, and today scientists predict with pinpoint accuracy the exact time and place of the occurrence of asteroids passing Earth, solar and lunar eclipses, and a vast variety of astronomical phenomena. In fact, it is due only to such predictability of behavior on such a cosmic scale that both the clock and calendar exist.

On the Earth, the gravitational pull of the moon causes the ocean tides to ebb and flow daily, like clockwork. Greek philosopher Aristotle and Roman historian Pliny the Elder commented that the brain was the "moistest" organ in the body and thereby most likely to be influenced by the moon.

Since the human body is nearly 80 percent water, it is within reason that the moon might affect our behaviors and even our nervous system. Recall, she wasn't named "Luna" (as in lunatic) the Roman goddess of the moon by accident. In fact, belief in the "lunar lunacy effect" existed in Europe throughout the Middle Ages. Even today people believe erratic behaviors, suicides, emergency room visits, bar fights and all manner of strange events tend to occur when the moon is full. It may be anecdotal, but every time I witness dangerous and aggressive driving I start looking for the full moon.

Now, just for "fun," consider astrology, widely regarded as a "pseudoscience" that originated a few millennia B.C., and is fundamentally based upon our unique relationship with the universe (position of the sun, moon and major planets) at the specific time of our birth.

While nearly all scientists are quick to dismiss astrology, a handful believes its consistencies for predicting personalities is undeniable. Kary Mullis, 1993 winner of the Nobel Prize for Chemistry, is one such individual. In his entertaining book *Dancing Naked in the Mind Field*, Mullis recounts how he became intrigued with the concept of astrology and pondered just how his brain might have any way of knowing the location of planets long before learning how to use a Nautical Almanac.

Whether you believe in astrology or not, the lesson to be heeded remains consistent: The same laws that govern the heavens must influence our behaviors. While this might suggest we are an effect, the real message is not one of surrender, but of responsibility and appreciation. With such an understanding, any redirection of personal energy allows for a new behavior to be born – launched into orbit at any given time (in keeping with the cosmic metaphor).

The truth is, on a multitude of levels, the majority of the universe and planetary behaviors demonstrate a predictable rhythm that is as unknowable as its very existence. However, understanding its mysteries is *not* the main objective: Working *within* the constructs of these universal laws to facilitate our personal objectives and desires is.

THE HABITS OF NATURE

"Cosmic habit-force is the greatest of all natural laws. It is nature's comptroller through which all other natural laws are coordinated."
- Napoleon Hill

Patterns are constantly created and recreated everywhere throughout life. The desert winds generate patterns in the sand dunes, schools of fish organize to precision, a low-pressure storm creates a perfect spiral, even ice crystals and molecules have perfect symmetry. When it comes to storing all of life's essential coding, even the DNA/RNA structure assumes a crystalline form.

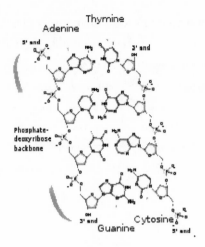

As an inherent part of this grand universe, can human behavior really be any different than its creative essence – those forces that lie above and within us?

Ultimately, it is this rhythm of our daily behavior patterns (our habits) that unleashes the same force and long-term effects that determine not only our current condition, but ultimately, our destiny.

What is more powerful than that?

After all, this may put an end to the nature-vs.-nurture debate, as the answer can only be *both*.

Over the years we have discovered some fantastic patterns within nature – habits, if you will. For instance, from the smallest microcosmic subatomic particle to weather patterns and even intergalactic space clusters, basic patterns and fractal structures exist – these are based on consistent numbers and dimensions. And the amazing thing is, all creations organic and even inorganic appear to follow these basic patterns. So if you know what to look for –

these key fractal patterns — you can see well beyond the *billions* of trees to see a forest. And what is revealed is one grand, underlying *unity* hidden deeply beneath the exterior diversity.

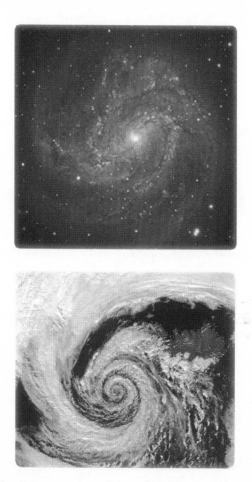

[M83 Galaxy (above) and Low Pressure Over Northern Hemispher]

Mark Barr, an American mathematician, used the Greek letter Phi (Φ) to represent the golden ratio, representative of the Greek sculptor Phidias who used the golden ratio in his works.

The golden ratio is an irrational mathematical constant with a value of approximately 1.6180339887; this is closely related to the famous Fibonacci sequence of numbers, each of which is the sum of the previous two, namely:

1, 1, 2, 3, 5, 8, 13, 21, 34, 55, 89, and so on.

The mathematics of the golden ratio and of the Fibonacci sequence are intimately interconnected – the ratio of each successive pair of Fibonacci numbers becomes closer and closer to the golden ratio. (For instance, 89 divided by 55 equals 1.6181, and the ratio keeps getting closer as the numbers increase.)

The Fibonacci numbers and golden ratio patterns occur so frequently in nature they are often referred to as a "law of nature." In other words, these numbers and ratios are nature's numbering system and are identifiable in all living things, from a single cell to a hive of bees and, of course, even humans.

Research suggests that these patterns serve various functions. For plants, such an arrangement supports survival and helps them grow efficiently by creating more space for the leaves or by improving the amount of light. Even a tiny advantage can help a plant survive and thrive within its environment.

The shell of the chambered nautilus reveals golden proportions. It too has a logarithmic spiral. *(Notice the remarkable similarities of the Nautilus, The Galaxy and the Low Pressure Storm [images above]).*

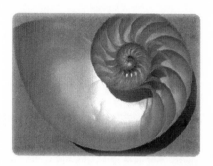

Sunflowers, for example, have a golden spiral seed arrangement that maximizes the number of seeds that are packed into a seed head.

Humans exhibit the Fibonacci characteristics, as evidenced in the proportions of the human finger, hand and arm. To get a quick visual of this, make a fist, hold it vertical and look down upon it as though you are trying to peer inside (you will again see a Nautilus-type spiral). Even the inner ear's cochlea forms a golden spiral. In fact, you'll notice that most of your body parts follow the patterns of one, two, three and five. You have one nose, two eyes and two ears, three segments in your arms and legs, and five fingers on each hand.

Simply put, the Fibonacci sequence and the golden ratio are manifestations of the universe's own habits.

In nature we see a predictable consistency – a sort of harmony throughout the universe. This harmony means a consistent, orderly fashion of each component contributing equally. Putting into practice the golden ratio – nature's empirical formula of intelligence, efficiency and balance – it is as though we are advised to follow the same model of equanimity. To do everything in moderation and avoid extremes: to seek equilibrium, harmony and balance in all our affairs.

PATTERNS OF LIFE AND ALCHEMY

*"No great discovery was ever made
without making a bold guess."*

- Isaac Newton

Alchemy refers to an early form of investigation into
nature and an early philosophical and spiritual discipline that
combines the studies of chemistry, metallurgy, physics,
medicine, astrology, mysticism, spiritualism and art all as
components *of one greater force.* Alchemy was practiced
throughout the world, in China, ancient Egypt,
Mesopotamia, Persia, India, Classical Greece and Rome,
Muslim civilizations, and in Europe through the 19th
century.

Alchemy was a key predecessor of modern sciences, and
many of its ancient processes continue to influence modern
chemical and metallurgical industries. Today, alchemy is of
interest chiefly to historians of science and philosophy, and
for its esoteric and artistic aspects.

While alchemy lost favor to other developing sciences,
it's important to note that the first physicists from a few
hundred years ago, such as Sir Isaac Newton, were
invariably alchemists. Leonardo da Vinci found it important
to master art, science and medicine all at the same time. Da
Vinci's story becomes a bit more fascinating when you learn
of his reported and unusual polyphasic sleep habit. Such a
manipulation of his own circadian rhythm most likely kept

his brain waves (more often than most) at or near the Alpha-Theta level (subconscious), and it stands to reason this may account for his remarkable insight, intuition and creativity. We'll revisit theory about creative insight later. For now, here's a chart of the different brain wave signals.

Brain Waves: Delta, Theta, Alpha, Beta, Gamma

Frequency Range	Name	Usually associated with:
> 40 Hz	Gamma waves	*Higher mental activity, including perception, problem solving, fear, and consciousness*
13–39 Hz	Beta waves	*Active, busy or anxious thinking and active concentration, arousal, cognition*
7–13 Hz	Alpha waves	*Relaxation (while awake), pre-sleep and pre-wake drowsiness*
4–7 Hz	Theta waves	*Dreams, deep meditation, REM sleep*
< 4 Hz	Delta waves	*Deep dreamless sleep, loss of body awareness*

During the Han dynasty in ancient China, a Sage was regarded as a wise person who could decipher, identify and master patterns. Upon reflection, this certainly makes a great deal of sense. Just yesterday, I walked out of the office (after being cooped up all day); as soon as I felt the crispness of the air I said, "Wow, September is here." This wasn't an insight that came from looking at a calendar; it was an instantaneous knowing grounded upon years of experience living in this climate.

In surfing, it's the experienced surfers who appreciate the important nuances that affect wave quality: tide, type of break (point, reef, beach), and wind (onshore, offshore, side shore), to name a few. When I first learned to surf, none of these important factors made any sense. Only the veteran surfers could decipher that important information (patterns) and recognize whether the waves would be any good and which locations would be the best.

Chances are, if you are considered a subject matter expert (wise in your craft), you recognize and appreciate far more subtle patterns and nuances than others. (As you read this book, I fully expect *your first impulse was to go straight to the Application section.* This "esoteric stuff," these nuances, probably may not mean much to you. However, as your sensibilities grow to the *subject* matter of habit, this natural *pattern* of behavior, I'm hopeful you will want to revisit this important section.)

Strangely enough, since I've become so observant of habit, I've even noticed how "tuned in" my dog is to my behavior patterns. That is, she watches me intently, "listening" to all of my non-verbal cues – each move I make. Depending upon the energy patterns (time of day and what I'm doing), she predicts when it is time to go play Frisbee or go for a walk.

Do not think for a minute such habit communication is relegated only to the animal kingdom; people innocently "speak" habit all the time. In fact, chances are that the better you are at recognizing subtle non-verbal habit cues, the more successful your interpersonal relationships are. Non-verbal communication reportedly accounts for upwards of 90 percent of all our interpersonal communication. So, it's this sort of understanding of non-verbal cues that triggers our internal "gut" feeling when a person is telling us one thing, yet their body language demonstrates something altogether different.

In fact, excelling in any subject or industry requires the keen ability to quickly recognize patterns – to adapt and evolve. Such adaptation presumes the ability to process and adjust. Recall Lao Tzu's profound statement: "The highest form of man is he who adapts."

One can adapt only when one recognizes patterns. Consider nature's ultimate adaptation machine: the chameleon. This creature immediately assumes the surrounding patterns dictated by the environment. And, don't forget Darwin's equally powerful statement on the matter, "It is not the strongest of the species that survives, or the most intelligent, but rather the one most adaptable to change."

So, whether it is communication, weather, economic, health or relationship patterns, the ability to identify and adapt appropriately becomes its own essential and fundamental habit. This applies to individuals, companies and societies.

Now, consider how appreciating the subtle nuances of habit *(as a master achiever might)* can help you radically improve your future achievements.

WELCOME TO YOUR MIND (WHICH IS NOT YOUR BRAIN)

Habit: The Language of Creativity and Achievement

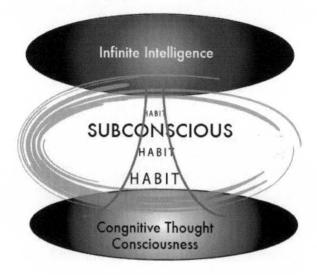

Infinite Intelligence

HABIT
SUBCONSCIOUS
HABIT
HABIT

Congnitive Thought
Consciousness

© 2010 • The Habit Factor®

*"There is a power above and behind us and we
are the channel of its communication."*
~Ralph Waldo Emerson

As reviewed previously, the brain can be seen, pointed
to and even, in scientific terms, measured. The mind, on the
other hand, cannot be seen, measured or even adequately
defined. How the mind relates to habit, creativity, intuition,

insight and even synchronicity demands further investigation.

Just what is the human mind?

While I have no evidence per se (recall Pascal's quote regarding reason, "an infinity of things which surpass it,") I will offer this theory: The *mind* consists, at least in part, of the energy fields (intelligence) connecting the heart and the brain. As we know, each organ's health is measured scientifically with electrocardiogram ECG (electrocardiography) and EEG (electroencephalography).

Humans are special beings in that our minds work at two distinct levels. We have the instinctual, habitual mind (subconscious) along with the rational, intellectual mind (conscious). In actuality, these are not really two unique and distinct parts, but rather connecting pieces of a fascinating and complex instrument.

Your **conscious** mind is your awareness. It thinks, reasons, calculates, plans and sets goals. Typically, it compares what we are experiencing with what we've experienced in the past, analyzing and dissecting problems we face and trying to come up with solutions to these problems. The conscious, intellectual portion of your mind makes hundreds of decisions every day, ranging from the mundane, like what to have for lunch, to the more important, like how to pay off a loan or solve an unexpected problem at work or school.

Your **subconscious** mind is where your past experiences exist. Your feelings, beliefs and values all make up your subconscious. Have you ever noticed the way you do things without even thinking about them? How you act reflexively, such as pressing down on imaginary brakes in a car while you are in the passenger seat? Have you ever been startled or jumped when you caught your own reflection in a mirror out of the corner of your eye? That was part of the instinctive fight or flight response that originates from your subconscious mind. Nothing was really there, but your mind and body responded as though you were under attack.

Your conscious mind is working only when you're awake; when you sleep, your conscious mind rests, but your subconscious, on the other hand, never sleeps. It is always on, quietly working in the background like a computer, ready to take over when your conscious mind fades out.

Such mysteries of the mind might also help explain the phenomenon of déjà vu, which literally means "something already seen." You feel strangely like you have been at a certain place, even though you've never visited it before. You find yourself knowing something that has not yet occurred. It's been reported that nearly 70 percent of the population has had some form of déjà vu, with the highest number of déjà vu incidents occurring in people aged 15 to 25 years old. Even science has not found a way to accurately explain why déjà vu happens, but one could hypothesize that it shares the same unconsciousness realm in which our habits exist.

Circadian rhythms, too, are another esoteric mystery. The actual word circadian comes from the Latin *circa diem*, which literally means "around a day." But circadian rhythms do not have to be daily, however, and can actually occur in multiple periods per day or during timeframes that exceed multiple days.

Obviously, we all know about sleep as a circadian rhythm, but other examples include menstrual cycles, body temperature, blood pressure, and the production of hormones and digestive juices. These circadian rhythms are not unique to humans, but are part of the makeup of many other organisms, with the simplest being the lowly cyanobacteria.

We know that our circadian rhythms are controlled by a biological clock, a sort of circadian pacemaker, if you will. This "clock" resides in the brain and is called the suprachiasmatic nucleus, or SCN. The SCN is located in the hypothalamus above where the optic nerves cross; it contains about 20,000 neurons. Its proximity to the optic nerve explains its reaction to light and by extension its sensitivity to times of day.

Birds are another creature whose lives are ruled by circadian. When it comes time for birds to perform their annual migrations, they are signaled by natural patterns. Scientists theorize that the change in temperature along with a change in the length of day have some effect, along with internal communication that signals birds to migrate. Birds also have an internal GPS that helps them navigate. Scientists say birds' navigation signal appears on first flight, but is then further honed over time as the bird continues to adjust to its environment. Therefore, a mixture of external and internal stimuli (energy) *communicates* to the bird that it is time to migrate.

Circadian rhythms fit the profile of habit when viewed through a human prism. The brain accepts inputs along with the signals it generates to create an output that is repeated over and over again. What is left unexplained, however, is this: Are circadian rhythms controlled by the brain or the mind, or a combination of the two? In the case of animals and instinct, it would appear a supernatural connection is intact. And, what of organisms without brains who possess circadian rhythms? Cyanobacteria lack brains, but still respond to circadian rhythms. What they don't lack, of course, is *energy*.

RHYTHM AND SONG

"Music in the soul," Lao Tzu once said, "can be heard by the universe." Reflect upon this once again: If the universe is one song, *rhythm* must be its language. Rhythm, in all its different forms, speaks to the universe and connects us with this vast system of intelligence. The intelligence, or power, Emerson proclaimed is "around and above us."

Perhaps this universal language of rhythm and song is best illustrated by the way some entertainment icons – particularly music artists – have such massive gravitational pull across vastly different cultures all over the world. Fans in Japan and China were mourning when Michael Jackson died, right alongside those in the Western world. Why does Jackson, or any other great artist, possess such massive, global appeal? The answer is they transcend cultural boundaries because song and music is an international and *universal language.*

Rhythm and song also tap into the realm of the *spiritual* – our connection with the universe. Churches sing hymns, African tribes chant … not only do rhythm and music create a setting of comfort and familiarity, but more importantly, they are a form of communication, a means for humans to tap into our creative and spiritual source – the supernatural, God, Infinite Intelligence – whichever term you prefer.[9]

When you take a closer look at music, it too has its own predictable structure, including melody, harmony and lyrics. The French composer Edgar Varese referred to music as "organized sound," which rings true because it seems to embrace practically anything that is labeled music, which anyone might conceive of as music, and undoubtedly anything that might be called music in the future. The most primitive musical note might be best recognized as our own rhythmic pulse, our own heartbeat. Picture an early caveman banging objects against each other in an early discovery of rhythm.

There is a strong sense of predictability in music that appeals to us on a fundamental level. This is why you don't need to understand the words – a beautiful tune is something everyone can appreciate; it sticks in your head and keeps you humming it all day. People all over the world are able to recognize the opening bars of Beethoven's Fifth Symphony. Music has always been a part of the human experience.

It is conceivable that song originally arose in human culture by imitating the songs of birds. The songs of birds appear to not be learned behaviors, but are perhaps hardwired into the bird's brain. In the human species, however, few things come hardwired, and one of them is our inclination to see, impose and create patterns whether they are musical or behavioral. So, while we are not hardwired with habits themselves — we are hardwired with the *ability to create our habits*. This is a miraculous gift, whether we appreciate it or not.

---

[9] To standardize this term moving forward, such references will use Napoleon Hill's term, Infinite Intelligence.

OVERARCHING ARCHETYPES

*"A good idea is never lost. Even though its
originator or possessor may die without
publicizing it, it will someday be reborn in the
mind of another..."*
~Thomas Edison

Carl Jung expanded upon Freud's theory of the
unconscious mind and imagined a greater "collective
unconscious," which consists of both the instinct and
experiences shared by all of humanity. By collective
unconscious, Jung is referring to the part of the psyche that
is never conscious. It is called collective because it is
universal, not individual.

Since the dawn of mankind, we have created a world of
symbolism. In fact, our symbols help to explain the world
around us, our relationship to the universe and seemingly
everything in between. The collective unconscious, Jung
says, is an instinct to which all of humanity is connected. It
is a shared repository of universal information, symbols and
archetypes.

As a psychiatrist, Jung's theories were based upon the
study of the human psyche and what function archetypes
play in our conscious state. Through his studies he
identified several important themes, which he discussed in
his book *The Archetypes and the Collective Unconscious.*

Interestingly, Aristotle brought up a similar point in his discussion of archetypes as related to moral virtue. Aristotle observed that while intellectual virtue primarily originates in teaching, "Moral virtue comes about as a result of habit." Such virtue is not something we are born with; individual habits, such as lying or honesty, are not naturally a part of the fabric of our identity. In Aristotle's words, "We are adapted by nature to receive virtues and are made perfect by habit." Such moral habits are not acquired via intellectual commitment, but rather by actually performing these habits.

According to Aristotle, ultimately, we condition ourselves via our habits. Over time, these habits become our "second nature" and forge our character, which ends up modulating and conditioning our emotional condition. The net result is that we gain more pleasure from moral action than immoral action.

CREATIVE INTELLIGENCE

The concept of creative intelligence began to gain traction only in the 1970s and '80s, when theories about intelligence were beginning to evolve. Speculation was that creative intelligence acts in harmony with other abilities to help us attain higher levels of achievement.

Many people are aware of the importance of creativity in creating success and even ensuring survival, but very few know how to ignite this power within themselves. Great artists and geniuses like Leonardo da Vinci, Thomas Edison, Picasso, Mozart, Charles Darwin, Einstein and William Shakespeare are but a few classic examples of supreme creative intelligence.

At a certain point, according to Malcolm Gladwell in his bestseller *Outliers, A Study of Success*, IQ becomes far less important (around 130), and your achievement or success is tied to many other variables. Mr. Gladwell astutely identifies such variables as income, culture and birthdates, to name a few, and I would humbly suggest that creative intelligence is another important factor – perhaps one of the most important, since it represents the ability to tap into an infinite realm of creativity and wisdom. (Mr. Gladwell clearly applied a great deal of creative intelligence when formulating and writing his books.)

Recall it was Einstein who said that, "Imagination is more important than knowledge." Although he never reportedly took an IQ test, his genius was highly regarded.

So, we can presume he said this with the understanding that knowledge is, for the most part, static. That is, if you were to line-graph **knowledge** and **imagination** on a horizontal timeline with the present (now) in the center, you'd notice that knowledge would fall to the left, and imagination would be on the right. This (the right side of the line and, coincidentally, the right side of our brain) is where the future resides – within our collective imaginations.

Naturally, those who work to master their creative intelligence rely on their intuition more often, are more confident about which goals to go after and are more in tune with a "calling" that leads them to new pursuits and passions. Interestingly, they also appear to be best in tune with when to rest and recharge, as creativity demands energy.

"Energy is bliss," William Blake once said. Keeping in mind that everything is energy, you can be sure that anytime senses are triggered, at the most basic level, energy transfer has taken place. "Nothing happens until something moves," Einstein often pointed out. Energy is always in effect within our surroundings. Hence, you'll notice that the Chinese art of Feng shui is essentially the art of skillfully optimizing the circulation of this energy (Qi). And since we are a form of energy, it becomes much easier to see the interplay between our habitual thoughts, actions, feelings and even creativity as they relate to our environment – our habitat.

Throughout time, we can trace an evolution of consciousness, from small breakthroughs to a progressively larger and more complex awareness. There seems to be a perpetual drive that compels us on, upward a spiral of expanding consciousness toward collective wisdom. There appears to be an innate need (collectively) to evolve to ever more expansive and integrated fields where knowledge, information and wisdom become unified. And that's what creative intelligence is about – engaging your whole being, appreciating and integrating *all* aspects of life. Consider the aforementioned creative geniuses; each had a major discovery or significant breakthrough by integrating "unrelated" subject matter. For instance, Picasso attempted to capture time on a two-dimensional canvas. Einstein applied thought experiments related to the nature of light, which led him to his theory of relativity.

So, it becomes rather apparent that true intelligence isn't the ability to regurgitate information. Real intelligence is identified through applied imagination and curiosity, where circumstances are turned into opportunities through explored and unlimited possibilities. Ultimately, it is creative intelligence and adaptability, not static knowledge, which serves as the highest form of intelligence. This is where opportunity and value reside in abundance.

The conscious and the subconscious, by definition, must overlap. To experience one you must experience the other. And, it's at that point, the intersection, where one becomes the other and vice versa, where our mortal realm touches the stuff of our very own creation; this is the source of our intuition. And this is where we will endeavor to journey in the next section.

The Esoteric, Precepts
(Ideas and Principles for Action)
Ideas

- Everything is energy.
- The same laws of energy that create the predictability of planets' movement affect our personal energies.
- The human body is mostly fluid, and the brain is the "moistest" organ in the body, which may account for theories like the "Lunar Lunacy effect."
- Appreciation of the cosmic forces helps us to better understand our natural behavior (habits) and how to best guide them.
- The disorder in the universe underscores our ability to create new behaviors and forge new habits.
- There are examples of habit patterns throughout the natural world.
- The mathematic constant of the golden ratio represents a unity of patterning and structure underlying all living things.
- Alchemy and the art of combining knowledge was a precedent to many sciences today.
- Your mind is in part the electromagnetic frequency/communication between the heart and the brain and unifies the fields of intelligence.
- Circadian rhythms are automated cycles of physiological behavior dictated by natural cycles.
- Music (rhythm and song) taps into the spiritual realm and transcends cultures. Music is a language and contains predictable structures.
- Theory: da Vinci's sleep habits likely kept his brain waves (more often than most) at the Alpha-Theta level, connecting him more frequently to insight. Consider his diagrams of the helicopter (more than 400 years before the first helicopters took flight).

Actions!

∞ What are the general patterns/conditions of your Mind, Body, Social, Spiritual and Financial Habits? Grade each with a (+) or (-) next to each to call attention to it.
Example: Finance (+), Body (-)

∞ Give each of these associated environments a score based upon current effectiveness and results (1-10, 10 is highest. For instance, Mind=8, Body =7, Social = 8, Spiritual=6, Finance=9. This is a quick, subjective way to further identify which areas need the most attention.

∞ Rate your personal feelings and attitudes, energies (thought habits) with a (+) or (-) next to each major category. For instance: Finance (+), Mind (+), Body (-), Social (-), Spiritual (-).

∞ Begin keeping a log or journal to specifically track when and where insight strikes most often. Example: April 25, 2010, idea for ad campaign while brushing teeth. This will help you identify what activities might be triggering this insight. Recognizing these cues can help to foster your creative intelligence.

HABITS: THE INTERSECTION

Intersection

- to cut across or through, overlap
each other.

American Heritage Dictionary, © 2009

---

*"The intellect has little to do on the road to
discovery. There comes a leap in consciousness, call it
intuition or what you will, the solution comes to you
and you don't know how or why."*
~Albert Einstein

INSTINCTS VERSUS HABITS

Instinct is the *inherent* inclination of a living organism toward a particular behavior. These inclinations or fixed-action patterns are unlearned and inherited. Instinct can be identified as an action performed by a creature, especially a very young one, without prior experience. When such behavior is performed by many similar creatures in the same way, without conscious knowledge, it is usually said to be instinctive.

Instincts are behavioral *patterns* that are not learned. They transpire in an almost-finished form even the first time they are ever executed. Examples include roosters crowing at sunrise, bats feeding at night, sperm whales migrating south in the winter, and sea turtles returning to the very same beach they were born to lay their egg. Think about the cuckoo migrating to lay her eggs in other birds' nests, and even humpback whales singing. Human babies have the instinct to suckle to find milk or sucking their thumbs to pacify themselves.

Habits differ from instincts, but only slightly because they are *learned.* To elaborate, every animal at birth takes food instinctively; however, no one can ride a bicycle naturally without being taught. Riding a bike is a learned skill. Yet once a person has ridden a bike for a while, the talent becomes so effortless it appears instinctual.

The process of learning, which is essential in the acquisition of habits, has been extensively studied in various animals. Here's one scientific example: You put a hungry cat inside a cage with a door that can be opened by pushing on a latch, and then put some food outside the cage. The cat, at first, darts around the cage making frantic efforts to force a way out. Finally, perhaps by accident, the latch is pushed and the cat pounces on the food. The following day you repeat the experiment and the cat gets out much more quickly. By the third day the cat escapes even more quickly, and finally, after a couple more days, the animal goes straight to the latch to exit.

This example effectively identifies two provisional laws of "acquired behavior or learning," in essence, scientific descriptions of habit formation.

The Law of Effect: Of several responses made to the same situation, those that are accompanied or closely followed by satisfaction to the creature will be, other things being equal, more firmly connected with the situation, so when the situation recurs, those responses are more likely to recur. Conversely, responses that are accompanied or closely followed by discomfort to the creature will, other things being equal, have their connections with that situation weakened, so that, when the situation recurs, those responses will be less likely to occur. *The greater the satisfaction or discomfort, the greater the strengthening or weakening of the bond.*

The Law of Exercise: Any response to a situation will, other things being equal, be more strongly connected with the situation *in proportion to the number of times it has been connected* with that unique situation and to the average vigor and duration of the connections.

What is true of animals, as it relates to instinct and habit, is equally true of humans (note the term "creature" above). The higher our mental faculty, the greater becomes our power of learning, and as a result some consider instinct to be less important in the life of man than for animals. This, however, would be misleading, since learning a habit is possible only when instinct supplies the initial driving force. The cat in the cage that gradually learned to get out performed the random movements at first due only to pure instinct. Similarly, children learning to walk at first make all sorts of movements, initially instinctive, beginning with crawling. These instinctive actions lead to experience, which becomes stored and either repeated or avoided based upon result (see The Law of Effect).

Habit can be any thought or behavior that is repeated frequently enough to become automatic and almost effortless. Even highly developed *social skills are habits* that are acquired through repetition. Conversation, as an example, is refined through considerable practice. You could even argue that love, respect and even integrity are nothing other than advanced socioemotional habits. Recall it was Aristotle who postulated that, "Moral excellence (virtue) comes about as a result of habit."

Charles Darwin noted that habits easily become associated with other habits, and once acquired, they often remain constant throughout life. For instance, when repeating a familiar song, one instinctive action often follows another in a sort of rhythm; if a person is interrupted in the middle of a song or in repeating or reciting anything by rote, he is generally forced to go back to the start to recover the habitual train of thought. My wife can recite two songs naming each state and president; however, if she's interrupted at any point in the midst of either, she needs to start from the beginning. So, depending on what elements might be there when you learn a particular skill (sound or smell, for example), eventually any similar encounter might trigger the memory or behavior, making it either easier to recall or perform. In March 2007, German researchers found they could use odors to activate memories of people while they slept, and the subjects even remembered better later.[iii]

Instincts might help habits develop, but *habits can become contagious.* An angry outburst is a good example. When you witness a child throwing a tantrum, you can be assured that there wasn't much learning that drove such behavior. However, as a child grows up, chances are she is exposed to other creative ways to express anger. Over time, those emotional outbursts became refined as a sort of habit, originally driven by instinct. Next time you get frustrated and really, really angry, chances are very good that your reaction may mirror the behavior of a parent or mentor and how they reacted when frustrated or angry.

This is interesting for at least two reasons: As the highly emotionalized state of anger draws upon and associates more powerfully with the other senses to reinforce the neural pathways of the subject, the observer is often affected. So, as a child, if you see a routine outburst repeatedly, the emotionalized energy strengthens its relationship within you, the observer, increasing the likelihood that you'll mirror this behavior as you mature.

We may not be able to alter our instinctive behaviors all the time, but often we can short-circuit them and inhibit the bad habits they help to create. For instance, if you have an instinct toward angry outbursts, it doesn't mean you must automatically have a habit of angry outbursts. You do have the ability to create new habits that prevent you from losing your temper.

The other day I found myself with a pair of pliers in my hand, but the job I was about to perform clearly called for a wrench. Not taking the time to find the right tool, I flailed about and became frustrated. After at least 10 minutes of struggling, I became angry. I caught myself, recognizing that my daughters were standing right next to me. Although I wanted to throw the pliers and shout a few expletives, I simply put the tool down and decided to take a little walk. The frustration triggered the onset of an outburst of my own, perhaps having witnessed similar outbursts as a child. Fortunately, I could see where this was heading and managed to find a little presence of mind.

I returned and, with a regained perspective on the situation, found myself laughing. All I was trying to do was adjust the seat height on my daughter's bike. But my hard-wired reaction nearly allowed this little episode to throw me way off balance.

FIND THE PARADOX/FIND THE TRUTH

We live in a world that separates and labels everything:
up/down, wet/dry, soft/hard, strong/weak, ugly/beautiful,
success/failure, male/female, happy/sad, start/finish,
life/death, rich/poor. And, there is nothing necessarily
wrong with this, as labeling helps us define things and
certainly helps us to communicate. Where we often can get
into trouble, it seems, is when we get stuck on labels or
even rules that appear hard and fast. Whenever we entrench
ourselves within such "knowledge," we fail to recognize the
fluidity and dynamism of life: Not only do opposites help to
define each other, perhaps more importantly, they contain
the seeds of the other. The iconic Chinese Ying/Yang
symbol encapsulates this precept. The little dots of
opposing color on each side represent the "seeds of the
opposite" and serve to remind us never to be deceived by
only what we see.

Since we've all been mentally conditioned from birth to
identify and seek separation, duality becomes this terrific,
all-pervasive illusion perpetuated throughout our
upbringing. We are conditioned from birth and through our
education to constantly seek opposites and not unity. In
other words, if a kid tells me how fantastic the rain is
because it makes him appreciate the sunshine, I'll fall over.
Now, I've heard adults say just that, displaying, of course, a
more real, holistic viewpoint refined by maturity.

So, as we more closely inspect our conscious being, we recognize it cannot operate without our subconscious playing a role. The subconscious and the conscious are part of the same unity. Yet, interestingly, when it comes to the study of intuition it's fascinating that science continues to search for the "part" of the brain where insight comes from, when naturally (literally, naturally) it's almost certainly of the very same source that created all life (the non-physical realm).

So, let's revisit Einstein's quote (this is perhaps the smartest man who ever lived wrestling with the concept of insight): "The intellect has little to do on the road to discovery. There comes a *leap in consciousness*, call it intuition or what you will, the solution comes to you and you don't know how or why."

How fascinating is that? Einstein chose the words – a *leap* in consciousness. I'd suggest to you that is precisely what it is, a literal *leap*, a connection to a higher form of consciousness: the superconscious or Infinite Intelligence via our subconscious.

So what is it? What provides this spark of insight, intuition, wisdom, or as Einstein put it, this "leap in consciousness?" I can only offer this theory: Human insight is a direct result of a connection to Infinite Intelligence. Recall Emerson's statement, "There is a power above and behind us and we are a channel to its communication." This "channel" occurs most often when you transcend your conscious being, even momentarily, and enter the subconscious mind.

Of course, one of the surest ways to enter the subconscious mind is *via habit*. (This might be any habit you may have that shifts your brain wave activity – napping, driving, rowing, jogging or showering, etc.). It is at that moment of complete relaxation (and release) when your creative mind and Infinite Intelligence as a "host station" *connect* (via the subconscious—*where habit lives!*) that you become a receptor!

Consider all those habitual activities you do: driving, showering, shaving, brushing your teeth, etc., and you're certain to notice a recurring pattern of insight during those times. They may not be insights that will change the world, but they do come from nowhere. You might find yourself driving, for instance, and then receive insight into a new headline for your AdWords campaign, or perhaps you were in the shower and realized the best way to market a new product was by establishing a never-before-considered strategic relationship!

Sleep is a perfect example of a habitual, rhythmic activity that facilitates insight. Sleep allows the opportunity to enter and exit the Alpha-Theta level of brain-wave activity. When you lower and harmonize both your heart and brain-wave rhythms (and related electromagnetic energies), the theory is that your mind becomes more attuned to creative insight and Infinite Intelligence. A quick example: Just last night I awoke at 3:45 a.m. with, of all things, an alternate kickoff strategy for our girls' youth soccer team. I am not sure where the thought came from, but I do recall prior to going to sleep contemplating how we might benefit from a different tactic.

The best part is, once you've identified your optimal insight patterns and practices, you can intentionally call upon them by deliberately seeking answers. You are likely familiar with the passage in the Bible, Matthew 7:8, which states, "For everyone that asketh receiveth; and he that seeketh findeth; and to him that knocketh it shall be opened." Once you submit your inquiry (persist with any question) and then via habitual activity enter the realm of subconsciousness, you detach and insight becomes possible.

Thomas Edison's insight for the light bulb came after numerous prior "failures." However, after arising from one of his famous catnaps[10], he was struck with insight: the image of hot coals buried underneath the dirt burning much longer than the other coals because of their lack of oxygen. That was it! A vacuum was required to keep the light bulb's filament from burning out too quickly. Another example: Paul McCartney cites a dream about his mother inspiring the song "Let It Be." Einstein reported that the Theory of General Relativity came to him in a dream. And, interestingly, in Mr. Gladwell's *Outliers,* he mentions Chris Langan, a man whose IQ was recorded at 195, and on other tests was deemed to be "off the charts." Mr. Langan shared that when it comes to identifying solutions and *receiving* insight to solve problems; all he has to do is go to bed

---

[10] Theory: Frequent naps for Edison (like da Vinci) kept brain waves in the Alpha-Theta level, enabling greater insight. Edison has over 1,000 U.S. patents to his name.

focusing on a particular question. Then, when he awakens, the answer is there nearly every time

I'm certain the vast majority of creation, insight and intuition accounts can be traced to similar episodes of detachment via the subconscious. In fact, the majority of this book and its own various insights about habit (and insight itself) have come while driving, surfing, jogging or cycling. I believe strongly, at that moment, when you release your conscious mind, typically via habitual activity, that synchronicity, insight and intuition most often strike. This is because habit (as rhythm) has served as both a language and conduit to Infinite Intelligence.

Synchronicity, which translates as "together time," was first identified by Carl Jung as a type of coincidence that was not just the result of unplanned events, but could be *intentioned* through coordinated thoughts (energy). As you stand in front of a mirror, you see your reflection. This is your physical reality. Synchronicity, though, allows you to look beyond the mirror to perceive another force (a different energy), and most importantly to trust in your ability to communicate your intentions. It is "here" that you momentarily transcend space, time and causality. This takes us well beyond our natural freedom of choice to put us hand in hand (finger to finger) with the creative source itself.

ONLY FIVE WATTS

"The successful man is the average man, focused!"

~Unknown

If you had to think creatively or conscientiously about each and every action, you'd likely be so mentally exhausted that you might have to sleep every few hours. Try this as an example: Focus on and be conscious only of your breathing. Feel your lungs inflate and deflate. Do this for two minutes with your attention squarely on your breathing. (Please put the book down.) Chances are good two minutes felt like 15, and time appeared to have slowed down.

What did you notice about your attention? Where was your energy at that moment? If you concentrated upon your lungs inflating and deflating, chances are good that you could literally think or focus upon nothing else. That sort of attention and focus captivates you in the literal sense; you are bound by it.

In fact, focus is one of the most powerful instruments we have, since focus channels the singular power of our energy. When used strategically, focus can help us achieve remarkable results. It's been said that a five-watt light bulb can barely light up a closet. Yet, that very same energy (five watts) when concentrated and *focused into a laser beam* can cut through steel.

Consider that if habit is "10 times nature," and you have the power and focus to craft your habits in the right way, you can literally create a *weapon of mass achievement* second to none. This, of course, is the same weapon the great achievers of all time have applied: *carefully refined habits applied with focus that compound over time!* No "secrets" here.

With applied focus and consistency, your actions are compounded favorably – *over time*. And, unfortunately, that is a horrible understatement. In fact, it's almost incomprehensible to understand the compounding effects of consistently applied action and focus. **Here's a quick example of a small action compounding**: Locate a piece of paper (doesn't really matter what size), and please try to fold it in half eight times. Now remember, this is just one small action applied consistently over time. What happened? Well, for starters, chances are you couldn't fold the paper more than seven times. Each successive action built upon the prior and transformed what was once a weak, thin and vulnerable piece of paper into a thick wad that seems unbreakable! This comes from just one small action building upon previous actions.

Similarly, when you set aside 15 minutes a day of reading and studying any subject (in your "spare" time), it can equate to a master's degree or even a Ph.D. in a given subject matter over the course of several years. Unfortunately, that same 15 minutes a day spent watching TV translates to *38 days'* worth of watching television (24 hours a day) over the course of 10 years[11]. And that's only 15 minutes a day! How much TV are you watching? Chances are excellent you *will* get a lot done if you redirected those "insignificant" 15 minutes.

Is it unsafe or unwise to watch TV? Not necessarily; for many people TV is used to decompress and relax. Groucho Marx used to say that he found TV very educational. That is, whenever the TV was turned on, he'd go into another room to read.

The caution is not against any particular action, but to be aware of the potential long-term benefits or consequences of any repeated behavior – over time.

Napoleon Hill famously pointed out that we all have the same 24 hours a day. Eight are devoted to sleep, which is relatively unalterable for proper health, and eight hours are devoted to our profession (assuming we're employed). Hill's point was to concentrate on those "other eight" hours and apply them toward your ambitions, dreams and desires. How those other eight hours are spent is what separates the achievers from the non-achievers.[12]

We all seem to understand the compounding effects of our actions; yet, nearly everyone undervalues them. In fact, it's rather typical to find people who *overestimate* what they can achieve in the near term, say one to three years, and *underestimate* what they can achieve in the long term, say 10

---

[11] According to a Scientific American article dated 2002; the average *daily* television viewing is three hours.

[12] This book was written in those "other" eight hours.

to 20 years. All great achievers (and great companies) seem to merely hit their stride 10 or, more often, 20 years into their endeavors. The Chinese have a wonderful proverb, "The best time to plant a tree was 20 years ago; the next best time is now." You may also recall Monty Hall's classic, "I'm an overnight success; it just took 20 years."

Empty-mind meditation is another useful tool you can apply to enhance focus. The practice trains you to observe and control your thoughts and emotions. Why should this matter? To begin with, all habit is originally conceived as a pattern of thought and must therefore involve energy and space. By ceasing all action/behavior and even thought, you take possession of your mind by simply emptying it. This allows for a refilling of the mind with purposeful, focused attention and intention.

Ironically, it is that same type of attention and focus that makes meditation so liberating for people, since we live mostly in a world of scattered, fragmented multitasking, where our actions are often started and many times rarely finished without any real presence or focus. "To be everywhere is to be nowhere," Seneca once wrote.

There is a great story of an old Zen master who continues to pour hot tea into his student's cup, even as it overflows and spills. The student jumps up and yells, "Master, my cup is already full!" The master then looks at the student sternly and nods his head. "Excellent. Then you do understand. I cannot add to your cup if it is already full."

By hitting the reset button and finding emptiness and silence via even simple and quick mediation, you can reset your emotions, clear your thoughts and intentionally drive new behaviors and habits with focused purpose and intention. Otherwise, if you fail to purposefully rest, relax and meditate, you are left with the same self-perpetuating cycle of activities that yields the same limited results. Unfortunately, we all know people (perhaps very close to us?) who continue to perform the same routines in a frenetic manner, producing, of course, the same limited, scattered and disappointing results.

Empty-mind meditation is a natural form of meditation; it is neutral and free of the different spiritual teachings and dogma, so anyone can practice it comfortably. By emptying the mind and becoming relaxed through breathing, you alter your consciousness and enter a realm of pure stillness and silence. It is here that you will find authentic wisdom and personal insight. "Silence," says a German proverb, "is a fence around wisdom."

In times of confusion or unrest, I used to respond immediately either emotionally or based upon fear (due to lack of information). However, for the last several years, rather than taking action I remind myself to remain still. This I gathered largely from Lao Tzu's sage advice, "Muddied waters left to stand become clear." Stillness and non-action allow for the information (energy) to settle, which then produces clarity. Stillness and non-action enhance focus. If you watch Olympic athletes prior to competition, you'll see they remain still and focused. This helps them visualize and channel their energies (their whole being) with laser-like focus.

Here's a fantastic technique you can use immediately to dramatically improve your focus and productivity: Get a timer and set it for 30 minutes. Commit yourself to working only on a single task during these 30 minutes. By doing this, you immediately filter out all other distractions. No phone calls, no e-mail, no Web surfing, etc. By "single-tasking" and focusing exclusively on the objective at hand, you will immediately see productivity gains and begin developing the *habit of focus*. As you find the strength of your focus improving, you can boost your single-focus time from 30 minutes to 40 or more. Do this incrementally.

Earlier, we introduced the concept of Qi (chee), the Chinese term for energy). An example of Qi application is to simply close your eyes and concentrate your attention (focus) upon your right hand. Then move your focus to your right index finger and maintain that focus for about a minute; hold it there and continue relaxed breathing. After a minute or so, keeping your eyes closed, shift your focus to your left hand and then to the index finder. Concentrate on the very tip of the finger. You will notice a remarkable sensation, a sensation that undeniably proves the age-old adage, "energy flows where your attention goes."

When this energy is channeled strategically – be it toward a new project for work, an essay for school or even training for a marathon, you can achieve remarkable results, given that this channeled energy remains consistent over time. This is where the habit of focus comes into play.

Consider once again that only five watts, when *focused into a laser*, can cut through steel. Repeated focus, then, applied toward any objective helps to forge the habits necessary to achieve any goal more quickly. The lesson is that it is not necessarily about the amount of energy that makes the difference, but the *quality of focus that is applied to the available energy, over time.*

The most outstanding entrepreneurs I know adhere strictly to this philosophy of focus. Since ideas are limitless, many entrepreneurs are often tempted to jump from one idea to the next (I must confess to this sin). Yet it's the focused person or entrepreneur with singular intentions who achieves his goals more often, with greater success at a much faster rate.

I experienced this lesson firsthand a couple of years ago when trying to establish a new, complementary IT software company closely related to our existing services business. The idea was to diversify our existing offering by specializing in a growing vertical market. Unfortunately, we attempted this at one of the most inopportune times, the beginning of a recession, and our splintered attention between the two companies proved almost fatal to both companies. My partners and I learned a tough lesson and agreed to proceed again only once we had a well-defined, more cautious path where our energies matched our newly defined priorities.

Reflect upon this for a moment: "If actions speak louder than words, *just how loud do your habits speak? And to whom?*" By persisting in our efforts habitually, we all have the ability to tap into the same natural flow of creative energy – the same power that keeps planets in perfect orbit.

So now is a good time to consider just how well your habits of thought and action *align* with your existing goals and intentions. Why must they align, you ask? Here's Brian Tracy's wonderful analogy explaining the importance of alignment: "Just as your car runs more smoothly and requires less energy to go faster and farther when the wheels are in perfect alignment, you perform better when your thoughts, feelings, emotions, goals and values are in balance."

THE BUSINESS OF HABIT

> *"The individual who wants to reach the top in business must appreciate the might of the force of habit – and must understand that practices are what create habits. He must be quick to break those habits that can break him – and hasten to adopt those practices that will become the habits that help him achieve the success he deserves."*
> ~J. Paul Getty

Most successful businesses now appear to get it. They recognize the undeniable correlation between human nature and purchasing habits. That is, they have now tied the success of their next product either to existing habits or, incredibly, the ability of the new product to create new consumer habits.

Seemingly every day new products are launched into the marketplace and now, finally, advertising campaigns have found the real bull's-eye – the habitual mind. In fact, this new "marketing science" has even been labeled "neuromarketing" as understanding deepens about customer behavior and the influence of habit in purchasing decisions. This means that while marketers in the past spent billions on advertising and customer loyalty programs, their efforts, unfortunately, were directed toward the wrong mind. They were attempting to win the conscious mind, but it's the unconscious, habitual mind that drives almost all of what we do and buy.

Dr. Gilbert Clotaire Rapaille has made a fascinating second career out of his specialized knowledge of human behavior. Originally a teacher at Sorbonne University, he ran private practices as a psychoanalyst and psychotherapist. Today, he's known within Detroit's inner circle as the "car-shrink," and has worked with the big three automakers GM, Ford and DaimlerChrysler. As a consultant, he's been credited for design innovations including the Hummer and PT Cruiser, as well as many others.

Rapaille's marketing insights stem from the Truine brain theory originally postulated by Paul D. MacLean[13]. The theory, in simplified terms, proffers that there is a third region of the brain in addition to the cortex and limbic regions called the "reptilian brain." Rapaille believes this is

---

[13] Recall the limbic brain from the Scientific Section.

the source of our primal, instinctual programming for two essential concerns: reproduction and survival. This region, he suggests, is accessible only via the subconscious mind. His main assertion is: There is a persistent three-way battle between the cortical, limbic and reptilian regions of the brain. His mantra is, "The reptilian brain always wins."[iv]

So, it becomes clear that professional marketers and consultants understand the importance of communicating successfully to the habitual, subconscious mind, and this has forced numerous companies to radically rethink their strategies. The astute companies now focus on behavior and habits rather than market research and customer surveys, which only access consumers' conscious desires.

Over the past decade, many companies have perfected the art of creating habits among consumers, whether it's via snacks, lotions or cleaners. Using a few principles of behavioral training, consumer psychologists have determined that: 1) It is most important and effective to market to behaviors instead of attitudes or beliefs; 2) Habit formation requires repetition/reward and cause/effect elements; 3) To enhance loyalty and/or increase purchase frequency, it is best to remove executive/conscious thought from the equation; 4) To steal consumers/clients, you must break or alter existing habits.[v] (While many debate whether Googling is a verb or not, I'm of the opinion that it's a habit. If you consider Google's dominance and the current search engine wars, the above habit-formation principles become particularly interesting. Thus, the more frequent and longer a habit remains in place, the stronger the habit. Good for Google; not so good for the competition.)

Apple's iPod and now iPhone are fantastic examples of how intuitive user design integrates snugly inside the habitual mind, thereby freeing the executive mind. Who doesn't want their mind "freed," particularly when trying to figure out new gadgets? Such an intuitive user interface quickly fosters habit development, which in turn strengthens brand loyalty.

Similarly, Nintendo introduced its Wii gaming console, shipping nearly 45 million units worldwide in only two years. Even though Nintendo was a pioneer in the gaming industry, it was losing market share to Microsoft and Sony (and their Xbox and PlayStation video-game consoles). Nintendo's executives seized a golden opportunity and created a game controller that integrated naturally with the player's instinctive movements; using the Wii controller became second nature. Whereas the competitors' consoles often challenged the player to look away from the TV and toward the controls, thus, jeopardizing their success in any given game.

On the flip side, the same sort of psychological understanding is helping to drive new, positive public-awareness marketing campaigns. One notable example is the "truth" campaign to help people stop smoking.

The "Truth" ads by the American Legacy Foundation show grotesque images, such as a hemorrhaging brain or inflamed heart, with text explaining that cigarettes are the cause. One ad dramatically directs a human-size rat surfacing from the subway station to a crowded street where bystanders are looking aghast. The rat (person in rat suite) collapses right on the sidewalk and holds a sign that reads,

"There's cyanide in cigarette smoke same as in rate poison."[vi]

A study by the American Legacy Foundation showed that 22 percent of the overall decline in youth smoking from 2000 to 2002 was attributable to its "Truth" campaign.

HABIT IN THE COMPANY CULTURE

You'll notice that businesses either spend millions to create successful employee habits on the back-end (think franchises training workers), or they spend millions on the front-end to identify prospective employees who will fit their culture (think interviews). The interview process is ultimately a matter of sifting through a person's past performance and character (habits) to see if they share the same values as the company (habits of thought and action by existing management and employees).

Knowing how important habit is to a company's success, it's curious to have never heard an interviewer ask, for instance, "What are your five best habits?" or "What are your two worst habits?" For the last few years, I've found it very useful and insightful to ask both. Ultimately, as it relates to a company's objective (determining a candidate's fit within its culture), there really may not be a better couple of questions to ask, at least initially. I recently received an e-mail (quasi-spam) from a company promoting business consulting services. The title of the e-mail was, "Aligning behavior with company goals, the key to successful change." To their credit, they are one of the few who have this correct. However, how interesting would that e-mail be if the title read, "Have you identified what core behaviors your employees must have to achieve your company goals?"

So, let's consider what might happen when you ask a prospective employee: *"Jim, can you share with me what you consider your five best habits to be?"* Now assuming he answers truthfully, you'll be provided some quick insight into whether Jim will fit into your company's culture. If Jim looks at you with a slight head tilt or seems a bit caught off-guard (and chances are he may), this could indicate he's not very conscious of his habits or maybe even is unaware that habit can be regarded as positive (which might tell you all you need to know about Jim).

Now, consider if Jim replies thoughtfully, "Well, I eat an apple a day, I don't watch more than an hour of TV, I try to make it a habit to read to my kids at night, I make it a habit to be punctual, and I try to read something related to my trade every day." Wow! By analyzing those answers, we quickly determine that Jim: 1) cares about his health, 2) is diligent with his time, 3) regards family as important, 4) is responsible, and 5) is an active and constant learner. Sounds like a high-quality candidate. In a matter of less than 10 minutes you've been able to identify his character. I'm not suggesting the interview should end there, but this is a fantastic way to augment your typical interview process. From my experience I reduced interview times by about one-third and ended up with better-quality employees.

All successful businesses demand consistency of either service or product. If you look at it from the consumer viewpoint, anything inconsistent takes the consumer out of "habit mode" into conscious, executive and "taxing the brain mode." Consumerism as an offshoot of human nature demands familiarity. Hence, consistency from the business side is literally drilled into the behaviors of the employees, so whether it's Starbucks, McDonald's, or Federal Express, it will not matter.

When it comes to management, there are few behaviors more important than communication. At our company, we share a saying: "We can only fail if we fail to communicate." This is how we emphasize the importance of communication. Our priority is to communicate proactively, openly and effectively with our clients, vendors and employees. While this slogan is a bit of an oversimplification, it reinforces the importance of thorough, routine communication. And, coincidently, the best way to ensure effective communication is to communicate routinely or *habitually*.

To assist in all forms of corporate communications, a key technique is to employ *rhythm*. Verne Harnish, author of *Mastering the Rockefeller Habits* and known as the "Growth Guy," insists that all businesses, particularly high-growth companies, perform daily "huddles." Such a predictable occurrence of communication helps to establish a rhythm within the meeting itself and among the regularity of these meetings. Rhythmic (habitual) communication is vital in client communications, as well, and might take the form of weekly e-mails or monthly newsletters or even periodic client-review meetings (say quarterly or semi-annually). Harnish shares this: "To make more than just a lot of noise in your business, you've got to have rhythm ... in the nineteen years I've spent working with growing companies, the predictable winners are those who have established a rhythm and a routine of having meetings."

THE POWER OF AFFIRMATIVE THOUGHT HABITS

"We don't see things as they are;
we see them as we are."
~ Anaïs Nin

It is clear that we can see the world only from our own limited experience and perspective, which has a dramatic impact on the way we perceive things to actually be – our apparent "reality." This is an awfully powerful insight when considering our own personal realities. At some point, it's important to transcend our habitual thoughts and self-talk and recognize we are bound only by our own mental constructs. That is, in order to experience any positive change it is important to address the "we are" in Ms. Nin's statement. And, the "we are" is based upon our thoughts – the repeated thoughts that have deeply embedded themselves into our subconscious.

So when it comes to self-talk, there appears to be some logic behind the effectiveness of affirmations. Changing your language (internal and external dialogue) requires a shift in focus (directed energy) that alters your perception through repetition.

*"The body is the servant of the mind. It
obeys the operations of the mind, whether
they be deliberately chosen or automatically
expressed. At the bidding of unlawful
thoughts the body sinks rapidly into
disease and decay; at the command of glad
and beautiful thoughts it becomes clothed
with youthfulness and beauty."*
~James Allen, As a Man Thinketh

To further illustrate the effects of our preconditioned thoughts, consider the following experiment involving two groups of people. The first group was presented images of a beautiful young woman, and the other group observed an older, less attractive woman. Following the initial exposure, each group was presented with a fairly abstract drawing that contained elements of both the old and younger woman.

While each group was certain that it assessed the subsequent illustration objectively, they regularly identified the likeness of the image with that of the original image to which they were exposed. So, for instance, those who saw the young woman first identified a young woman in the drawing, and those who saw the image of an old woman recognized an older woman in the illustration.

Without any prior context, can you find *both* the young and the old woman?

Similarly, once we identify our own preconditioned, limited visions, we are open to expanding our abilities to envision new outcomes and horizons. Once we acknowledge our past mental conditioning or mental myopia, we are able to behold new paradigms of thought. In fact, this is really the only way anyone can advance beyond the realm of self-imposed boundaries.

Such a shift is a prerequisite to solve any current challenges or significant problems. Whether it is about achieving a goal or learning to think more creatively about a problem, altering and many times *erasing* prior conceptions is essential. This is very likely what Einstein meant when he commented, "We can't solve problems by using the same kind of thinking we used when we created them."

This psychological reframing is often catalyzed by new experiences and shared perspectives that help us to redefine just what is possible. For instance, if you think your business would be doing fantastic at $5 million in sales, and then you meet someone in the same industry doing $100 million, that's going to broaden your horizons pretty quickly!

I initially thought completing a marathon was near impossible; that prospect changed significantly when I was introduced to Ironman-distance triathlon events (which end with a marathon preceded by a 2.4-mile swim and a 112-mile bike ride), and now, to stay motivated while training for an Ironman triathlon (and to keep myself from complaining), I constantly remind myself of Dean Karnazes (ultramarathonman.com), who just completed 50 marathons in 50 states over the course of 50 days! Rest assured, that knowledge has radically altered my perception of what the human body can endure,

Whenever you're introduced to new possibilities, your frame of reference grows. Such a shift in viewpoint is similar to what many do when faced with difficult circumstances. Often a quick pick-me-up is to consider the other poor souls around the world who are much worse off than you. With that viewpoint and *thought pattern*, you're immediately reminded of just how fortunate and blessed you really are. The same perception and energy shift is a requirement to realize any significant mental breakthrough.

And, as you must know, the mental breakthrough always precedes any parallel physical breakthrough.

So, the more we can expose ourselves to new experiences and others' perspectives, the more rapidly we're able to redefine our internal preconceptions to create a more colorful world of possibilities. Such enlightenment is a given to a certain degree within our education system. As children we're exposed to various studies, from biology and music to math and science, broadening our horizons.

After school, however, many of us cease the active pursuit of new studies and new experiences, favoring what is known and comfortable. Many even flee to the comfort of old habits, old knowledge and old associations. The problem with this behavior is that we're rudely and inevitably confronted by two of life's great constants: change and time. Since habits reside only within the constructs of space and time, they demand change as well. By clinging to old habits (seeking comfort) and not accepting the realities of change, we unwittingly weaken the effectiveness of our old habits. We actually cling to an illusion of past effectiveness – something that has already begun to slip away.

When you are aware enough and appreciate the dynamism of life, you find yourself constantly crafting new habits designed to support your *future* visions and goals. *It's critical to be constantly designing habits today for the goals and ideals of tomorrow.* Thus, we recognize the greatest successes are always in a constant state of reinvention. Think about a success story you know. If that person or company is still relevant or enjoys the same level of success they experienced a decade ago, you can be assured they've reinvented themselves, perhaps numerous times.

To make the most profound and significant changes in our lives, we must get to work on the most basic and essential paradigms through which we see the world, our most primary, fundamental and repeated small actions: We must revisit our habits of *thought* that constitute our *beliefs*.

The Habit Factor reminds us that it's not just about a particular set of habits. **Habit is a language much like music is a language. Therefore, like music, it should be understood, appreciated, taught and mastered.** While there are thousands of hit songs, and thousands more to be created and there are even *formulas* for hit songs, the masters of music are the ones who understand music's underlying principles. Similarly, you can rest assured the masters of achievement understand the underlying principles of habit.

So, by going broader rather than deeper and studying the whole rather than its parts, we rightly put our emphasis where it should be: on the ultimate habit, which is recognizing, appreciating and mastering the language of habit *before* trying to master any specific set of habits.

VALUES AND PRINCIPLES

As long as we're talking about the principles underlying habit, now is a good time to try and clarify the difference between values and principles. The two are often interchanged and far too often misunderstood. Let's quickly review what they are and how they can help us fashion habits that are relevant to our success.

Principles are best recognized as inherent and natural governing laws and timeless truths, or, a truth that is the foundation for other truths. For instance, "maturity requires time," or, "experience is the best teacher," or, "health is your most prized asset," or, "the best way to treat others is how you'd like to be treated." The golden rule is a principle, and it's based upon a truth that is timeless and ultimately proves to be self-evident.

Values, on the other hand, are more personal and unique; they tend to be selected based upon what a person holds dear. One person may truly value money, while another might value family, or love or kindness.

A critical problem arises when values don't align with principles. If what you value is ultimately out of harmony with timeless truths, the principles prevail. If someone values money over health, health as a governing natural law will always be more significant, no matter how much the person values money or how much money she has.

Then, there is habit, which is energy automated and repeated in the form of *action*. Habits dance between these two powerful forces in human achievement: values and principles (much like it intermediates consciousness and the subconscious). If principles are timeless governing laws and values are what we cherish and hold highly, habits subconsciously connect us to each. It is interesting to note that while principles and values can outwardly influence your habits, it is your actions and behaviors (consciously applied at first, which become habits) that reveal your inner values and relationship to principles. In simple terms, how you act and think repeatedly displays your values and the principles you identify with, resulting, of course, in the composite of your character.

With an understanding of values and principles, applied awareness helps you to craft the habits necessary to achieve practically any new goal you can conceive. Aligning your habits with your values, for instance, can help you to direct your energies to serve those objectives. And, in the case of principles, this technique helps you to transform negative habits into positive habits, helping you to manifest new results far more quickly.

The principle of charity, for instance, comes to mind. Charity is a self-governing precept that says we are here to serve our fellow humans in some capacity. As a principle, service proves itself to be self-evident. Therefore, it's no coincidence that some of the most successful business executives I know serve on one or more nonprofit boards. From the outside looking in, this might seem like some advanced form of lip service until you recognize that charity fits tightly within the executive's value system and aligns with the principle of *serving*. Then, it becomes no strange coincidence that such charitable service ends up rewarding the executive in terms of goodwill, new associations, new friends and contacts, and perhaps even new business.

Each of us has hundreds if not thousands of habits in action each day. By intentionally crafting the most important ones with purpose and aligning them with your values and principles, you radically accelerate your success.

PRACTICE, PRACTICE, PRACTICE

"Excellence is achieved by the mastery of the fundamentals."
~Vince Lombardi

Legend has it Lombardi once welcomed his team of professional football players to training camp with the following exclamation: "Gentlemen," he said, waving a football before his team, "this is a football." A brilliant and dramatic way to ensure all his men understood that success begins with mastery of the fundamentals.

If you were to study first responders, emergency medical personnel, police and institutions such as the military, where people must react appropriately and *automatically* in times of extreme stress, you will see that it is *fundamentals repetition* that helps to ensure people are acting out of habit *instead* of cognition.

I had a conversation with a Coast Guard helicopter pilot, and when I asked him if flying a helicopter was hard, the answer I expected was "No, it's easy." What I got was, "It's F'ing hard!" That concerned me a little, so I asked him to elaborate. "Well, it *was* F'ing hard at first," he said. He went on to explain that between the communications device in his ear, the number of instruments he's supposed to observe, the sensitivity of the controls and the fact that he's supposed to be always considering various contingencies in advance, I began to get the picture. However, with The

Habit Factor in mind, I persisted and asked him about the amount of simulation training he must have had prior to actual flying. He then explained that simulator training was essential and helped to ingrain the automated reactions necessary when flying the helicopter.

Later on, he told me with pride about his commanding officer (who flew Marine One, the presidential helicopter), and recollected with awe that he was able to land the massive chopper within inches of a target and with such a delicate touch that the president's coffee wouldn't so much as shake. This too, he acknowledged, was a product of the habits developed through the repetition of practice drills (simulator and real life) over many years to make the seemingly impossible, at first, almost easy.

In sports, particularly championship moments, stress is extremely high. A notable example of this was in the 2010 NBA finals, where the Lakers took on the Celtics. If you witnessed this, you probably recall Ron Artest, a recent free-agent acquisition for the Lakers who delivered a below-average performance in game five of the best-of-seven series. When asked about Artest after the game, Lakers star Kobe Bryant suggested that Ron should rely on his natural, instinctive abilities (his habitual self), and said something like, "Sometimes Ron just *thinks* too much; he needs to just go out there and play like he knows how."

It's interesting to note that in the decisive game seven, it was Artest who kept the Lakers in the game and who was largely responsible for the team's championship win with what Coach Phil Jackson labeled an "MVP-type" performance. Coincidently, the first person Artest thanked, right then and there on the floor, was his psychiatrist, whom he acknowledged before the entire arena and a national television audience. Artest emotionally said, "I definitely want to thank my psychiatrist. She helped me relax – *a lot.*"[vii] It was a beautiful illustration of allowing the habitual, subconscious mind to take over in moments of intense stress to achieve high performance. This happens only when the fundamental groundwork – in the form of thousands of hours of practice – has been put into place.

Coincidentally, it should also be noted that to secure the game for the Lakers, critical free throws were made by Pau Gasol and Sasha Vujacic in the final moments, and those players are known for their European practice habits and solid fundamentals.

It is the same drilling of fundamentals that distinguishes great coaches from average coaches. On some level the very best coaches recognize that they are tapping into something far more significant when drilling the fundamentals. They are tapping into The Habit Factor, the unconscious realm (a ritual of pattern) where in times of intense pressure, when players are under incredible stress, it isn't cognition, but habit that ultimately sets them apart as champions. There is simply no time for cognitive thought in fast-paced professional sports. Recall the great Hall-of-Fame Yankee catcher Yogi Berra, who said, "Think? How the hell are you gonna think and hit at the same time?"

In the Netherlands, a youth soccer academy called Ajax is renowned for producing the very best soccer players in the world (not surprisingly, the Netherlands found itself in the 2010 World Cup finals and the 2014 World Cup semifinals).

One of the key premises of the academy's practicing technique is to focus more on the fundamentals and practice itself, and engage in fewer games than their counterparts in other countries.

Gregory van der Wiel, a recent product of the renowned system who was awarded the 2010 Johan Cruijff Award for "Young Player of the Year" in the Netherlands, had this to say about the Ajax academy's detail-oriented routine: "You do things again and again and again, then you repeat it some more times."[viii] Now, there may be no more eloquent way to convey exactly how to develop effective habits.

Mastery, at its core, is the result of developing and refining the essential habits of any particular skillset. Therefore, the highest level of performance or mastery in any endeavor involves mindlessness, or *unconscious* competence. In the 1970s, a man by the name of Noel Burch proposed the "The Four Stages of Learning a New Skill," or as often referred to today, the "Four Stages of Competence."[14]

His theory suggests that the highest of all skill levels is "unconscious competence."[15] This makes sense since, as we reviewed earlier, thinking is comparatively slow. This is why

---

[14] http://en.wikipedia.org/wiki/Four_stages_of_competence
[15] "True" highest level is an efficient and delicate dance between unconscious and conscious competence.

repeated drilling is what the military, police, first responders and sports teams do ad nauseam.

I know from personal experience playing and coaching kids on the soccer field, for instance, that the strongest players are the ones who are essentially without conscious thought, playing confident and focused – trusting the skills they've refined in practice. Unfortunately, the kids who struggle most often are simply *thinking too much*.

Thinking (under pressure) costs precious seconds, and in soccer results more often than not in losing possession of the soccer ball. "Get out there – you're playing fine … stop thinking and go play!" I assured a young girl on our team. An older sideline referee walked over and commented that he wished he had heard that advice more frequently from coaches to their young players.

Consider the journey of a hypothetical, great pianist. When she first learns, she is either unaware (*unconscious*) of how bad she is, or she may be aware (*conscious*) of her *incompetence* – either way, it is only through deliberate practice that she can move up to a slightly higher level of skill, known as *conscious competence*. At this level, she's better. She can play, and yet she still struggles; she isn't overly fluid or confident. It is only when she has put in thousands of hours (some suggest 10,000 or more[16]) that she'll reach the highest level of skill, *unconscious competence*, where the essential habits required for mastery are fully developed. Here the pianist is confident, focused and fluid. She is without reservation or conscious thought; her fingers move quickly and with ease, and she's consumed by her music.

The Four Stages of Competence theory has been amended a bit to even include a fifth stage, which varies by authors and is not part of the original model; however, the idea makes sense. Consider a great virtuoso, masterfully weaving between both conscious and unconscious competence levels and improvising based upon various situations, feedback or requests.

---

[16] This is elaborated upon in greater detail in the Application Section, Choice: The Ultimate Freedom.

HEALTH: BACK TO THE FUTURE

Below, for your consideration, here are the Top 6
leading causes of death in the United States[17].

1) Diseases of the heart	Heat Attack (mainly)	26%
(2) Malignant neoplasms	Cancer	23.1%
(3) Cerebrovascular disease	Stroke	5.7%
(4) Chronic lower respiratory disease	Emphysema, Chronic Bronchitis	5.1%
(5) Unintentional injuries	Accidents	5.0%
(6) Diabetes mellitus	Diabetes	3.0%

Of the top six, the first two, heart disease and cancer,
account for more than one-half of American deaths. (I

---

[17] (Source: National Vital Statistics Report, Volume 58, Number 14 [March 31, 2010] statistics for 2006.)

included #6 because diabetes is a growing concern in America and continues to rise due to our poor dietary habits as a nation.)

What does this have to do with habits? Only everything. Cancer and heart disease are directly tied to our diet and exercise habits. I'm not going to tell anyone what to eat or turn this into a book about diet and exercise. However, here's a quick story that perhaps many of you might be able to relate to.

A few years ago (just a few), I went to my 20-year high school reunion. It was terrific to see so many old friends, but it wasn't so terrific to see firsthand the compounding effects of some people's health habits, particularly in terms of diet and fitness. It was evident rather quickly who had adopted some positive lifestyle habits and who was neglecting their health. If I had ever doubted my decision to turn vegetarian 20 years ago (and I hadn't), this would have been all the assurance I needed.

As individuals, and even as a society, it seems we may be literally missing the big picture. Most people tend to view each dietary episode in a one-off fashion, as in one cheeseburger a day rather than 300 cheeseburgers a year. One quart of ice cream doesn't seem quite as damaging as the 100 pounds of ice cream a year that it adds up to be. Or, the one cigarette vs. the 30 cartons a year – or the 300 cartons over 10 years. The examples are many and obvious, but still it appears too many of us fail to realize the significance of the compounding effects of our dietary habits until it is too late.

Conversely, that one salad opted for at lunch can turn into 300 salads a year. An apple a day turns into 365 apples a year. The six glasses of water a day becomes 300 gallons of water a year. The bottom line is that maintaining a *long-term* perspective when it comes to our daily diet and exercise habits will yield incredible health benefits that literally keep us alive.

About three years ago I found myself visiting one of our best network engineers in the hospital. Unbelievably, he was being treated for an irregular heart beat and diagnosed with mild heart disease (at age 30!).Turns out, he had the habit of drinking about six cans of soda a day. Needless to say, this habit caught up with him.

With diet and exercise we seem to recognize the theory and importance of moderation. But it appears we all too quickly get sucked into the gravitational pull of our daily dietary habits, often without awareness of the ultimate outcome.

Can we get away with one ice cream or cheeseburger a week? Chances are very good we can. However, the counsel is to remain vigilant and at the same time cognizant of what the long-term effects of any one behavior might be – particularly should that behavior become a habit. It is important to recognize the tendency of any behavior (energy) toward routine, rhythm and, ultimately, habit.

The Intersection, Precepts
(Ideas and Principles for Action)
<u>Ideas</u>

- Habits are often contagious, passed from generation to generation.
- Habits are learned, and instincts are not.
- Separatism is an illusion; there is one source for all that is invisible and visible.
- A leap in consciousness is a result of the connection to Infinite Intelligence facilitated by the language of habit.
- A great way to call on insight is to ask the question you seek answers for, and then detach via habitual activity.
- Synchronicity and coincidence are examples of energy coordinated to assist our clearly stated goals.
- Focus is energy concentrated. A five-watt light bulb can barely light a closet, but when focused as a laser it cuts through steel.
- Empty-mind mediation allows for fresh ideas, providing focus.
- Successful businesses market to the habitual brain.
- Habit directly influences business success, as evidenced by franchises, value alignment.
- Shared information can alter perceptions and affects outcomes.
- What we "see" is largely based upon our prior perceptions formed by habitual thought patterns.
- To solve any significant problem, a shift in our "level of thought" or perception is required.
- Habit is a language much like music is a language and must be understood, appreciated and mastered.
- Fifteen minutes of focused and consistent behavior can equate to a master's degree or Ph.D. after a few years.
- By aligning our repeated actions (habits) with principles and values, we accelerate our achievement.

Actions!

∞   Can you list five *positive* habits you inherited from your family? Can you list five negative (or more?) *Which was easier to identify (the positive or the negative)?*

∞   List three ways you clear and reset your mind. Lao Tzu's advice is helpful here: *"Muddied waters left to stand become clear."*

∞   List any professional associations you have considered joining, but haven't. Example: Chamber of Commerce, Toastmasters, a local nonprofit group. Can you commit to joining such a group in order to create new associations and break through old, limiting behaviors?

∞   Identify a list of five values you hold dear. Now list five habits of *behavior* that would support each. Do you have these habits? Example: Value =Freedom. Associated Habit = Surfing.

THE INTERSECTION

HABITS: APPLICATION

> Application: The act of putting
> something to a special use or
> purpose: *an application of a new
> method.*
>
> American Heritage Dictionary, © 2009

"True life is lived when tiny changes occur."
~Leo Tolstoy

APPLICATION

The application of any knowledge is where the rubber meets the road, where theory slams head-on into reality. To know these powerful truths is one thing; to apply them becomes literally life-altering. As Anthony Robbins once explained, "Knowledge without action is only *potential* power." And, I'm sure by now you've come to recognize that the word "habit" implies *repeated action*.

To comprehend the power of habit and understand its significance is an important first step. But consciously crafting productive and supportive habits is absolutely critical for successful achievement. As we said from the start, it may not be easy, but it does get *easier*, over time.

Before you proceed further, *here's a bit of a warning.* **As rudimentary as the goal and habit-alignment process appears, please know this it is a practical, proven and effective process.**

I've often noticed that the most basic and simple strategies prove to be the most effective and even life— altering. I recommend you take the time to read each step of the goal and habit setup process thoroughly, and then fully set up one goal first, as this will help you to understand the overall process and will aid in the subsequent setup of goals at a later time.

The Habit Factor®
The Science of Behavior
Meets the Art of Achievement. ™
∞

Please follow the outlined steps below, and if you don't hit your goal, I want to know about it. E-mail me at mg@thehabitfactor.com

In fact, when you do achieve your goals, I'd love to know about that, too. Please consider copying the following pages ahead of time, as you're encouraged to write down your goals in the book. Or, visit www.thehabitfactor.com for templates and worksheets.

Create your goals and your ideal life – one habit at a time!

Find FREE templates, tutorials, updates and more at:
www.thehabitfactor.com
www.facebook.com/thehabitfactor

CREATE YOUR GOAL IN SIX SIMPLE STEPS

The process to set up a goal and its core, related habits is relatively straightforward. However, the system does require some thoughtful consideration, so each of the steps is first outlined and then explained in detail.

1) Identify the goal.

2) Specify the Start Date and *Projected* End Date.

3) Capture the "Why?" That is, why is your goal meaningful and emotionally significant?

4) Describe in detail what the goal looks like once it has been successfully achieved.

5) Identify Key Milestones in the journey toward your completed goal.

6) Habit Alignment. Set up core habits that relate to the achievement of your goal. This process has its own six steps:

   a. Identify core habits (between 3-5).
   b. Establish minimum success criteria for each habit.
   c. Describe why each habit is important.
   d. Identify Target Days of the week you will perform the behavior/habit.
   e. Establish the Tracking Period start and end dates.
   f. **TRACK!** (*Daily*)!

Step One: Identify and write out your goal:

You can't hit a target that you can't see, both literally and in your mind's eye. To see your target physically, <u>write</u> it down or <u>print</u> it out! To see it in your mind's eye, visualize it! *State your goal here:*

_____

_____

Step Two: Identify both the START DATE and the *projected* END DATE:

> **Start Date:** _____

> **End Date:** _____

Start Date: For purposes of illustration, we will assume your start date is immediate; however, in the event you are identifying a list of goals, you may have various start dates. In the interest of focus, you'll want to start with one goal.

End Date: While your goal may have a hard deadline, such as a marathon, it may also be something a little more amorphous, such as starting a business or raising $1 million dollars. In such instances, a best-case scenario should be considered as your end date. Note: It's important to recognize that the end date is a target, not an absolute. I've witnessed time and again where people miss their end date and become disillusioned and disheartened. Even the most precise achievers and companies miss their target end dates sometimes. Consider how many times NASA has had to postpone a shuttle launch. When NASA misses a target date, it doesn't scrap the whole mission; it simply sets up a new target end date.

The end date should always serve you and it should never discourage you. If you ever miss your end date, accept the lessons and be sure to appreciate and acknowledge the progress and successes you've encountered along the way.

Here's a quick example: I was coaching an executive who had the goal of completing a half-Ironman triathlon. To his credit, he recognized he was a little overweight and out of shape. He was working too many hours and wanted to establish this goal to create some balance in his life. He trained hard and became rather fit over the course of about three months. As the event date approached, he had to travel due to unexpected circumstances. This travel put him out of his training routine and he ended up missing the event. Rather than being upset or discouraged, he recognized the many successes he had along the way: He became fit, developed far better eating habits and enjoyed more energy and creativity (he also lost at least 20 pounds). He commented many times throughout the training that he was more interested in the process than the goal, and for this reason alone he was a success.

By recognizing that the real success lay in the journey and not the goal itself, he remained positive even after missing his goal.

When you view any experience this way, you quickly realize there are no mistakes, only lessons, and there are no failures, only experiences. *By the way, what is the only way to truly fail? Have you given any thought to what "failure" really is? I plan to revisit this a little later.*

Step Three:
Capture the "Why?" Then, visualize the successful result!

Identify why the goal is important to you, and be certain you can see its successful outcome! If you can't see the successful outcome, set a similar, smaller goal. For instance, if the original goal was a marathon and you just can't see completing it, aim for a half-marathon. If you can't envision that, aim for a 10K or a 5K. To start, it's important to identify a target that requires at least a little stretching beyond your comfort zone.

The "Why?" is designed for you to capture the emotion (energy) associated with the successful completion of the goal. What would it mean to you to successfully achieve your goal? Here's perhaps an even better question: *"What would it mean if you never achieved your goal?"* I've personally found that question and the associated emotions of regret and disappointment to be extremely motivating.

Capture Your "Why?"

As Roz pointed out in the Foreword, if the "Why?" is
meaningful enough, it will not only motivate you through
times of despair and challenge, but it also can light the way.
A meaningful "Why?" always contains within it insightful
strategies and tactics, as well as shear resourcefulness, to
help you achieve your goal.

Case in point, during her Atlantic crossing, all of her
oars broke – think about that! There she was in the middle
of the ocean and every oar she had was broken. Roz credits
her "Why?" for her determination and resourcefulness. She
identified her best alternative was to construct usable oars
out of the broken ones. For this, she used duct tape and
created splints from other broken oars. Now that is
resourceful!

Any goal worth pursuing will present seemingly infinite
obstacles, and the only way to counter those is with a truly
meaningful and personally significant "Why?"

When you emotionalize your goals, you can't help but to
visualize their successful achievement. Take time to use

your imagination and see your triumphant arrival within your mind's eye.

Step Four:
Describe the goal, and then identify what you are willing to exchange in order to receive it.[18]

Describe:

For instance, if your goal is to start a new business, describe it in great detail: "Develop an online retail presence selling not just computer systems but also consulting services for business intelligence and automation. Our ideal client will be…" As you write out your description, if it is a really tough goal, you will immediately notice feelings of anxiousness, anticipation, doubt and nervousness, perhaps even anxiety. These can serve you well! You are an emotional being and, when channeled and applied

---

[18] In the mobile app Steps Three and Four are integrated into one field.

constructively, these emotions provide the necessary energy that drives you onward.

Just be ready, as these feelings of doubt tend to be accompanied by a series of excuses, as in, "How are you going to run a marathon when you can't even run one mile?" Or, "You could never start an online business because you don't know anything about the Internet and you have family obligations and ..."

Know that the excuses will be endless. Choose not to accept them! Some coaches suggest you should ignore them, but my recommendation is to listen to them, gather the information, but don't let them dissuade you. For instance, "you don't know anything about the Internet" might be good information, but not entirely true. Chances are you know *something* about the Internet or you wouldn't have a goal to create an online business. The excuse in many cases may provide you with some constructive information. In this case, "Buy a book, or take a class to learn more about the Internet!"

If your goal is money related, it's recommended you identify what you are willing to give up/exchange in order to achieve your goal. Be assured that nothing comes without a price and money is sure to flow toward value.

What is value? Here's a simple formula: Value = Purpose + Creativity.

Purpose (solve a problem or serve others) + Creativity (How unique is your solution or service? What is your creative spin that makes it better, easier, faster?). This equals Value (something people are willing to pay for).

Value could be just doing your job very well or serving a purpose with greater creativity. The greater the purpose and applied creativity, the greater the value, thus, the greater the return.

You've probably recognized another term for money is "currency," and for good reason, as it is simply another form of energy that *flows* to where the value is (energy seeks its most efficient, shortest route, much like an electrical current, hence the term "currency"). Therefore, it's important to identify what you are willing to contribute in exchange for the desired finances to create value. Unless you are stealing money (not recommended), you ought to know money is always a result, a by-product of the value you provide and is not acquired directly (other than gifts). Identify a purpose (typically driven by passion), apply creativity, and watch the money (currency) flow.

Ask yourself now, how are you able to provide value and serve? Where do your unique talents and abilities lie? Answering these questions will help you become clear on how you will achieve your personal financial goals.

Step Five: Milestones

Break your big goal into substantial milestones. For instance, if the goal is to run a marathon by June 30, chances are you will want to be able to run at least half that distance halfway between the start date and the end date. If your goal is to have sales of a million dollars, the same general rule applies. One half the amount "X" by one-half the time "Y." How many milestones you establish is up to you; the least amount needed is recommended and ought to be tied to achievable bites that you can envision completing by critical dates.

Step Six: Habit Alignment Technology™

You don't get what you want; you get what you measure (TRACK!).
Identify and Align critical habits associated to your goals.

Habit Alignment is the most certain and fundamental of all roads to goal achievement. And, when combined with daily tracking, you are certain to realize immediate momentum. If there were only one thing you took away from this book, my hope is it's this:

> **When you conscientiously craft supportive habits that align with your goals and *then track them daily*, you achieve your goals faster and easier every time.**

ILLUSTRATION • Habit Alignment Technology™

Habit Alignment Technology™ for Goal achievement

STEP #1: IDENTIFY GOAL

Goal Name :

Run a Marathon

STEP #2: Identify Core, related habits
Related Habits

#1 **Drink Water**

#2 **Stretch**

#3 **Run**

#4 **Visualize**

#5 **Read related Material**

STEP #3: Identify minimum success criteria for each habit.

Drink _6_, 12oz glasses of water

Qty or Time (per day)

Stretch for _12_ minutes

Run for _20_ minutes

STEP #4: Identify **Target** Days for each habit.

Monday (Tuesday) Wednesday (Thursday) Friday (Saturday) Sunday

Example: Target might be every day for "drink water" while "Run" might only be 3 days a week.

STEP #5: Establish Tracking Period for Habits

Initial recommended Tracking Period for ALL Habits is four weeks

Another Example:

GOAL   **End Date:**
"Double product sales"   12/31/2015

Related Daily Habits	Min. Quantity/Time
Out of bed by 5:30 a.m.	(Quantity 1)
Network Market	(1 hour)
Read Trade Publications	(30 minutes)
Build Affiliates	(30 minutes)
Identify new market opps.	(30 minutes)

Here we've identified at least five critical, related habits that, if accomplished according to the minimum specified quantity or time and the identified Target Days (below), will help you to achieve the above stated goal.

You may be thinking, that's terrific for "Running a Marathon," but how might I apply The Habit Factor to "Starting a new business?"

Well, since we can agree that all goal achievement requires momentum, to begin, the first question you might ask is, what three to five behaviors (habits) could you start and track specifically related to the goal of "Starting a business"? Perhaps it's a daily commitment to "Networking" (for one hour a day), three times a week to build clientele and spread awareness of your services. Or, what about "Studying your field" of expertise 30 minutes a day), five times a week or, "writing your business plan" (one hour a day) three times a week or, "building the company Web site" 30 minutes a day), four times a week. Any or all of these habits, when tracked against your "Target/Ideal days of the week," would be incredible momentum builders! Plus, I'm certain that after only the first four-week tracking period you'd be so much further along than if you were to write out a bunch of action items or To-Do steps.

By applying this simple process, I've witnessed one entrepreneur double his sales in a year. He simply identified three important "sales tools" (as he called them) that were critical to growth, and he tracked them against his target days.

You may be saying, "I'm not looking to start a company or run a marathon – I'd just like to be a better, more productive employee." To that end, I will share that another executive sat down with one of his employees, an office administrator who was performing terrifically in almost every aspect of her job. However, she had an unfortunate habit of being late to meetings where she was supposed to be early and help prepare. At his wits end, he decided to share The Habit Factor worksheet with her. He even shared his own habits and targets in order to relate first how much the process helped him. (By the way, his sharing of his personal experience first is a stellar example of quality management.) They then agreed on an ideal target number of instances for the following month. Later he confided to me, "I tried literally everything I could think of with her – rewards, punishments, different systems, but I've got to tell you, this sheet, made such a difference. It's taken a couple months, but she has changed dramatically – she's not been late again."

As you begin this process, you will notice that there isn't
a goal that doesn't have critical, associated behaviors
(habits) that can be tracked against their ideal targets. So,
please understand, this process isn't just for paddling from
Catalina or rowing across the Pacific. The Habit Factor
works for *all* goals, since all goals can be deconstructed and
then, of course, reconstructed in the same fashion.

**Glossary of terms: Understanding the Nomenclature
and Habit Alignment Technology™ better.**

Frequency, Establishing Target Days

In the above example, Goal Example II: "Double
Product Sales," you see the habit, "Out of bed by 5:30 a.m."
The question I'm often asked is, "Does this mean I have to
be out of bed *every day* by 5:30 a.m.?" The answer is, "That is
up to you." In order to double your product sales, do you
need to be out of bed by 5:30 a.m. every day? And, perhaps
more importantly, is it *reasonable*? In other words, if you've
never been out of bed before 8:30 a.m., what are the
chances you're going to be out of bed by 5:30 *every* morning?

So the idea is to first establish a frequency of Target
Days (for each week) related to each habit that is *reasonable*.
The process allows you to increase the frequency in
subsequent tracking periods.

When you recognize that any day you are out of bed by
5:30 a.m. is progress, you might at first elect to start with
only three days a week versus seven.

Only you will know if you've set up a daily frequency
(per week) for each habit that is achievable and reasonable.

The beauty is that the process is designed for total flexibility, since once you've completed your first 30-day Tracking Period you can modify the Target Day frequency by adding more days within the week, or perhaps you may even need to reduce them.

In fact, this process not only allows you to increase the Target Days (strengthening the habit), but you can also increase the Target Minimums (per habit), as well. So, once you find that you've started meeting your "Network Marketing" Target frequency of three times a week, you might increase it to four or five times a week. Or, you can even up the minimum success criteria from one hour to two hours per instance. The entire process is flexible and at your discretion.

Target Days:
Example: **Tuesday**, **Thursday**, **Saturday**

Target days are essential to the tracking process, as these are the days you *ideally* choose to perform the habit. However, since you may recognize that due to existing obligations certain behaviors may be achievable only on certain days, you have the flexibility to establish select Target Days per habit.

In this example we have identified just three target days during the week, since we know, for example, that on Monday and Friday we most likely won't be able to perform the "Network Marketing" behavior. For each habit you identify the ideal target days that will provide you with both progress and momentum toward your goal.

Tracking on Non-Target Days:

Another important point is you have the ability to perform the habit on Non-Target days. Here's an example: We might be able to "Read Trade Publications" (minimum of 20 minutes) on Sunday; however, we choose not to make it a Target Day. By doing this, Sunday becomes *optional*. Should you find the opportunity to complete the behavior on Sunday (a Non-Target day), you still get to check it off (yes!).

The rationale is that by tracking the habit even on "non-target" days, you foster the habit of *tracking* (which becomes its own important habit), and you provide yourself with the opportunity for a "make-up" day should you miss a Target Day, allowing you to achieve your week's ideal frequency. Note: This added flexibility allows you to surpass your frequency targets during your tracking period. For example, you might have the frequency target of three days a week for network marketing, but you may actually perform the habit five times in a week.

Minimum Quantity or Time (per Habit)

Anytime you establish a key habit, the "Minimum Quantity OR Time" for each must be identified. This is the metric that allows you to know if you have successfully met your objective for the day. For example: If my minimum target for "Network Marketing" is "1 Hour" and I only spend 15 minutes performing the related behaviors, I would NOT give myself a check for the day -- not until I've reached my daily minimum for the behavior. This may sound a bit harsh, but according to this method you can get credit for the habit only once you've met the daily minimum quantity or time you've established for the habit.

TRACKING: Make Your Success Binary!

Once you've identified the key, related habits and established their respective minimum success criteria and Target Days, tracking the success of each habit is as simple as either a Check (YES) or No Check (No) for each desired behavior/habit.

This is another significant differentiator of The Habit Factor vs. other habit-tracking systems. Interestingly, other systems allow you to have multiple checks within a day for the same behavior. With The Habit Factor, your success is binary: It's either a YES or NO (per day) – a simple CHECK (Yes) or NO CHECK (No). The rationale behind this is significant, as it favors the *long-term perspective*. In order to develop any habit, *consistency* is the key, not multiple checks or points within a day.

Habit formation demands consistency over the long haul. Think about it; if you can have eight checks in a day, why couldn't you have 20 or 30? Where does it end, and how is that driving and serving the *long-term* development of the habit? Unfortunately, it doesn't, therefore it shouldn't be important. In fact, it's that sort of inequity of energy and effort that brings about subsequent lulls of activity. So, while multiple checks might be nice or make you feel good *temporarily*, rest assured, by keeping track of your progress at a binary level (YES/NO) you will develop the persistence required to mature any behavior into a habit over time. Once it truly becomes a habit, you will find you no longer have to Track it – hence The Habit *Factor.*

.

Tracking Periods:

The next essential element of the process is the Tracking Period. This is the period of time in which you will initially track your actual behaviors vs. your ideal targets for any one period (initially, four weeks is recommended). Tracking Periods[19] are required for habit formation and are entirely customizable.

At the end of each tracking period you can modify your Targets (by either increasing or lowering the frequency and minimums) based upon the prior tracking period's results.

For instance, my initial Tracking Period is going to be March 6, 2015 through April 7, 2015. My target days are Tuesday, Thursday and Saturday. This tracking period allows for a total of 14 Target days where I'm expecting myself to "Write for a minimum of 50 minutes a day." As mentioned above, this allows you to give yourself a YES (check) even on Non-Target Day within the period if you should perform the behavior. So, it's conceivable that if you are doing really well, out of the period's 33 days and 14

---

[19] The mobile app, by demand, allows for infinite tracking periods with no end date. However, it's important to use tracking periods to measure your progress and actual behaviors vs. ideals.

-

Target days you may actually write for your minimum of "50 minutes" on 14 or more days (say 18 days). This would put you at 128 percent for the Tracking Period and suggests that during the next Tracking Period you should increase the frequency target.

Conversely, if you were to score a 57 percent (only eight days out of the 14), you might want to keep the target days the same or may even decide to reduce them in the next Tracking Period. Again, this system is flexible at almost every level of the setup and tracking process and is designed to reward and encourage progress while allowing for modification and more reasonable targets if needed.

Be sure to capture the "Why?" for each habit during setup, as well.

When trying to establish a habit (much like the goal), it's useful to identify the reason you desire the habit and capture the emotional energy (the Why?). For instance, when setting up the "Network Marketing" habit, the "Why?" might be, "By establishing this habit, our sales leads will increase by three or four times over the next year." That's the sort of motivation that will keep you moving and tracking! Recall the late, great Jim Rohn's terrific quote,

"Motivation is what gets you started.
Habit is what keeps you going."

Setup Process Summary

So there you have it, six relatively simple and quick steps designed to enable your rapid progress toward goal achievement!

1. Name the goal.
2. Identify the goal Start and Projected End Date.
3. Capture the reason (identify why it's important/ emotionally significant).
4. Describe the goal in detail. (Visualize it and detail what it looks like when achieved.)
5. Establish significant milestones.
6. Identify, establish and Track core, related behaviors designed to create habits.

Habit Alignment Summary:

1. Identify Core, Related Habits (only 3-5!).
2. Identify Minimum Success criteria for each habit. (Quantity or Time minimums).
3. Establish initial Tracking Period (4 weeks recommended).
4. Capture the "Why?" for your related habit.
5. Identify the Target Days (per week).
6. **TRACK DAILY!**

Habit Alignment Technology™ for Goal Achievement

WORKSHEET

STEP #1: IDENTIFY GOAL

Goal Name :

STEP #2: Identify core, related habits

Related Habits

#1

#2

#3

#4

#5

STEP #3: Identify minimum success criteria for each habit.

Qty or Time   Qty or Time
(per day)

STEP #4: Identify **Target** Days for each habit.

Monday   Tuesday   Wednesday   Thursday   Friday   Saturday   Sunday

Example: Target might be every day for "drink water" while "Run" might only be 3 days a week.

STEP #5: Establish Tracking Period for Habits

Initial recommended Tracking Period for ALL Habits is four weeks

© Equilibrium Enterprises, Inc.

Habit Alignment Technology™ for Goal Achievement

WORKSHEET

STEP #1: IDENTIFY GOAL

Goal Name :

STEP #2: Identify core, related habits

Related Habits

#1

#2

#3

#4

#5

STEP #3: Identify minimum success criteria for each habit.

Qty or Time   Qty or Time
(per day)

STEP #4: Identify Target Days for each habit.

Monday   Tuesday   Wednesday   Thursday   Friday   Saturday   Sunday

Example: Target might be every day for "drink water" while "Run" might only be 3 days a week.

STEP #5: Establish Tracking Period for Habits

Initial recommended Tracking Period for ALL Habits is four weeks

The Habit Factor® Tracking Sheet

The Habit Factor

PERIOD:

Habit Names

GOAL:

DAY	Date	T	A	T	A	T	A	T	A	T	A	z	Comments:

Weekly SubTotal

Weekly SubTotal

Weekly SubTotal

Weekly SubTotal

GOAL:

TOTAL:

• Commited on: _____

• Sign:

166

The Habit Factor® Tracking Sheet

The Habit Factor◆

DAY	Date	T	A	T	A	T	A	T	A	T	A	z	Comments:

PERIOD:

Habit Names

GOAL:

Weekly SubTotal

Weekly SubTotal

Weekly SubTotal

Weekly SubTotal

GOAL:
TOTAL:

• Commited on: _____
• Sign:

167

A couple of Tracking modes from within the mobile app.

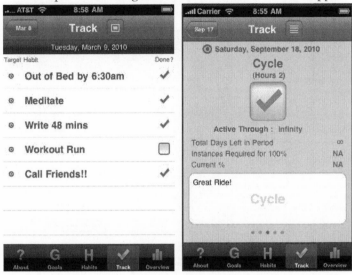

Habit Alignment Technology™ Charted, "Drinking water" Streak.
Goal is Ironman® Triathlon, with % of habits vs. ideals.

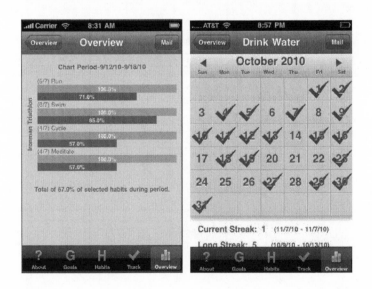

GOALS ARE NOT OPTIONAL

In life, please know that goals are not optional (period). Since you have made it this far, chances are that I'm preaching to the choir. Nonetheless, this is an important mindset to understand as well as share.

Jim Rohn summed it up brilliantly: "Here's really the goal of the human adventure [notice he said *goal*]: The full development of *all your potential*. That's the *goal*." I'm sure you recognize that the development of all your potential provides ample room for *many* goals. One goal may be to improve your service to others, another to refine your skills, another to lift more weights or run faster. The process for continual improvement is never-ending and should expire only when you do.

Unfortunately, goals appear to be optional. In fact, the majority of people do not consciously establish their goals and rarely do they write them down. "Why is it," Brian Tracy wonders, "people can receive a master's level of education, yet never have been taught even an hour's worth of goal-setting best practices?"

Stranger still, it appears there's a sort of movement or philosophy *against* goal-setting, as though goals could be bad for a person. I guess one theory is that by setting a goal, you're likely to fail to be fully present or appreciate the little time we do have in our life. I'd suggest to you, though, the opposite actually takes place. When you are without a goal, destination or direction, the moment actually becomes lost in a sea of other moments, directionless, aimless and, sadly, meaningless and unrewarding. Even with total presence, aimlessness serves no one. And when you are serving no one, you are not serving yourself.

I love this quip from the late inspirational columnist George Matthew Adams: "We cannot waste time, we can only waste ourselves." That is astute. Time is infinite, and becomes finite only within the context of our lives. We never actually waste time. Time could care less. However, without purpose we needlessly waste ourselves. Goals provide purpose and purpose provides goals.

You see, as a CREATure, creativity is your fundamental nature. I hope you don't doubt this, because too often people think they aren't creative. Simply reflect back upon your childhood. Perhaps you thoroughly enjoyed drawing, coloring, playing with Lincoln Logs®, Legos® or Play-Doh®. You were lost in time – captivated by the creative process. My daughters will play in the sand at the beach for hours at a time, building "castles" and "rivers" and "fish pools." Pablo Picasso once reflected, "Every child is an artist. The problem is how to remain an artist once he grows up." I'll never forget, at the age of six, how our daughter Mia couldn't get her paint and paper out fast enough. She'd just witnessed a magnificent sunset and told her mother, who wondered just what she was doing making such a mess, "I just want to paint that beautiful sunset Mommy."

I was in awe, realizing I just witnessed the presence of a force deep within her, *inspiring* her to create.

Know this: You possess this same power. You must.

You see, your characteristics (interesting choice of
words as it relates to habits) must mirror those of your
creative source, the source of all life. Notice Mia was
inspired, the Latin etymology of which is "inspirare,"
meaning literally "to breathe into, upon or in." In this case,
the energy and the vision of the sunset breathed into and
upon her.

Creativity, therefore, becomes both a responsibility and
an obligation for each of us. Beyond that, I'm sure you
recognize the significance creativity plays in your self-
fulfillment, self-actualization and happiness. It was Maslow
who postulated, "What a man can be, he must be." What
you can be is achieved only through the process of
creativity!

Goals are the equivalent of metaphysical super-glue,
bonding your creative essence to that of your birthright –
your dreams, ambitions and desires. Goals provide
direction, purposefulness and meaning. Aimlessness, on the
other hand, when constant and perpetual (typically over
years), results in personal tragedy, sadly, every time. There is
another paradox here, as *temporary* aimlessness often
provides relief, revitalization and a new perspective. Such
temporary aimlessness often reveals a new creative path and
direction. So, stepping off any given path, at any particular
moment, helps to shed light on new possibilities and
directions. The caution, however, is to beware of prolonged
aimlessness, which can produce no favorable result. All
great achievements are the result of a goal realized or a by-
product thereof.

In order to set goals, you must first tap into your creative essence, your core being, as well as your imagination. Notice the very faculty of goal-setting distinguishes us from other creatures on Earth. How many creatures are you aware of that set out to build skyscrapers and bridges or skydive, write books, create plays, race cars, compete in sports, make movies, etc.? Goals are the direct application of your creative faculties.

What's even more fascinating (and here is yet another paradox) is that a goal of not having a goal is, of course, a goal. The fascinating thing is everyone actually has goals; it just appears that some people have better crafted and well-thought-out goals than others. While one may have a detailed plan to complete a triathlon, or achieve a million dollars in sales or write a book, another might have a non-written or even unconsciously affirmed goal to simply "get through the day" or "make it through the week." Indeed, some goals are better conceived than others. Mark Twain often joked, "I can help anyone get anything they want out of life; the only problem is no one can tell me what they want."

So, now it's your turn. Have you identified what it is you really want? Do you have your goals written out, in detail?

Where is your ideal place to live?
What is your ideal career?
What do your ideal family and friend relationships look and feel like?
What does your ideal body look like?
What is your ideal occupation?

What is your ideal spiritual relationship?
What would be a significant goal if you could achieve it within a year?

Spend some time now identifying your goals – your ideals. Observe the tendency here to use the word "ideal." Anything that is ideal demands your attention and imagination, your ability to tap into your creative spirit. The word "ideal" forces you to think proactively and plan, creating a sense of responsibility. There is an infinite number of creative, goal-oriented questions you can ask yourself to identify your most meaningful goals. How do you know if they are your most meaningful goals? Compare them against your values and even against a personal mission statement, if you have one. I won't try to tackle personal mission statements here, since that can get pretty detailed. You can learn a lot about personal mission statements at FranklinCovey.

An even a better exercise I find myself consistently recommending to people is for them to write their own obituary. I'd first heard about the power of this exercise when I was told the story of Alfred Nobel, who was a Swedish chemist known for his invention of dynamite. The story reportedly goes that while Nobel's brother was visiting Cannes, France, in 1888, he died. Due to an identity mix-up, a newspaper erroneously reported that "The Merchant of Death is Dead." Alfred was shocked by such a negative recounting of his life and was determined to alter the legacy he would leave. Approximately seven years later he would sign over his estate's fortune (approximately $250 million worth in today's U.S. dollars) to establish the Nobel Prizes, awarded annually to individuals without regard to their nationality. Awards are given in the following categories: Chemistry, Medical and Physical Sciences, Literature, and to those furthering a mission of global peace.

We can all learn a great deal from Nobel's personal episode. Simply imagine you've lived a full, long life and have accomplished all your goals. By performing this exercise it instantly helps you identify just what your priorities are and how to best apply your limited time in this life. If done with great care and thoughtfulness, this exercise is sure to help crystallize your intended purpose and provide immediate direction in the form of short-term (six-month and one-year) and long-term (five- and 10-year) goals.

Coincidently, as you may have noticed in this book's Foreword, this is the very exercise Roz Savage credits with transforming and redirecting her life from one of a business management consultant to becoming the first woman to row across both the Atlantic and Pacific oceans, as well as becoming an advocate for environmental awareness. Talk about a radical transformation. Roz wrote two obituaries: one as if her life's career path didn't change, and another that represented her ideal obituary, how she wanted to be remembered. Her accomplishments in just a few short years speak for themselves.

Once you've identified that major purpose (theme), it's good to break your goals into representative categories (major pillars) to ensure wholeness and balance. Consider each of the following categories that directly influence your life: Body (health), Mind, Social, Spiritual, Financial,

Professional, Family, and Adventure (lifestyle). Then you can establish a priority based upon the urgency of each. It's important to limit the amount of goals you set in order to retain focus. As success and confidence build, you might be able to then work on a couple of goals in parallel.

WHY S.M.A.R.T. GOALS ARE *SLIGHTLY* STUPID

"Everything should be as simple as it can be, but not simpler."
~Einstein

When it comes to goal setting, it seems the majority of the Western business world and individuals adhere to a process known as the "S.M.A.R.T." goals system. In the event you have not heard of this methodology, it is simply an acronym that stands for Specific, Measurable, Achievable, Relevant and Time Bound. Each of the aforementioned criteria is important to address when a person or company formulates their goal. This system was reportedly introduced back in 1981[20]. While for the most part this has served as a fairly practical goal system, unfortunately, it completely fails to recognize the very important, HABIT-GOAL relationship.

Even today, you'll still find the vast majority of coaches and "success experts" missing the fundamental Habit-Goal

---

[20] 1981 by George T. Doran in the November issue of *Management Review*.

relationship and the basic importance of "**Habit Alignment.**"

Even Wikipedia's current entry[ix] on "Goal Setting" reveals *zero* references to "habit."

None.[21]

I fully recognize Wikipedia is not the end-all on the science of goal achievement, but I do think, as a collective, global repository, it provides a fair indication of the awareness of the general public as it relates to the subject matter. The screen shot below is the result of searching for the word "habit" within the Wikipedia "Goal Setting" entry.

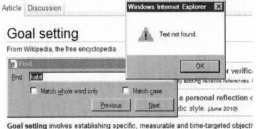

To further illustrate the continued misuse, nonuse and even confusion about habits and goals: I just ran across an article on a *coach's* blog who said, when trying to achieve

---

goals it is important to *"avoid habits."* He then went on to say, by habits "I'm referring to smoking, drugs and drinking." Unfortunately, this coach is still stuck with the old, negative connotation of habits.

So, please, if you plan on using the SMART goals system, at least promise yourself you will make the process **HAPPY**— a basic acronym designed to remind you about the importance of habit alignment: Be sure to track daily, relevant **H**abits that are **A**ligned. Ensure they have **P**urpose (they are core, important and related to the goal) and they are **P**ositive (don't ever track negative habits), and finally, be sure you celebrate any progress with a great big "**Y**es!" Or, a "yay," "yippie," or something that starts with a "**Y**"!

The Habit Factor marks a new era in the association and awareness of habit and its unique relationship to goal achievement. The simple truth is that any (*stretch*) goal is achievable once you *dissect* and identify its Key Habit Attributes (KHAs). Then, by tracking each KHA daily, you gain *immediate momentum*, which is a prerequisite for any goal to be achieved. We call this Habit Alignment Technology,™ and what makes it so effective is you don't need a long, detailed list of planned task or actions. You simply need to know the core, related habits (typically, no more than five to retain focus), and then realizing immediate results is nearly automatic!

Most (if not all) goal-achievement systems are designed in the following manner: You are asked to write the Goal Name at the top, and under that you're expected to identify and list your planned next steps/actions. This is essentially a very long task list of subsequent steps. I don't know about you, but this is where I got lost every time. How am I supposed to list the planned actions (perhaps hundreds of steps) for a goal I have never achieved? And, assuming I complete that task, where is my energy going to be by the time I'm done listing all of these steps? Chances are good I'll be overwhelmed by the enormity of it all. Again, this tends to be where my momentum would stop every time. On the flip-side, consider how much easier it is to simply track the habit, "Spend 15 minutes reading about topic X," and do that three times a week. Or, "20 pushups" four times a week. The Habit Factor allows you to *quickly plan and capture* the required time investment per day, as in, "15 minutes of reading" at a frequency of "X" occurrences per week. With the "SMART" system, the elusive "next steps" always left me wondering what happened next, and all too often left me stuck.

Unfortunately, this system for setting goals never did work very effectively for me, and now I understand why. You may wonder, "Well, how are you going to know what to do if you're only tracking the habit of "Network Market for 50 minutes?" The answer is, since you are tracking the amount of time spent, you will be *aware* of your actions (and have to fill that time); you will be in tune and will ask and quickly identify what the next steps are as required. Therefore, your planning takes place as you track – over time. This is extremely important and useful as it keeps the progress and momentum flowing in your favor. So, for instance, when a networking event presents itself, you enroll and attend because you recognize it will meet your ideal target of networking.

Another key differentiator is that The Habit Factor works *backward* from the goal as if it has been achieved. The SMART system, on the other hand, essentially asks, "What's the next step"? Here's an example with the SMART System. Goal: "Lose 20 Pounds by March 31, 2016." Next steps: Go shopping for low calorie meals, throw out bad food, renew gym membership, etc.

Now, consider The Habit Factor process, which begins *with the vision* of you already having achieved your goal. You actually start by saying to yourself, "Wow! _____(name), you just lost 20 pounds. You look terrific! *You must have had some incredible habits to make that happen!* **What were they?"** "Well," you say, "I tracked only three core habits. I stopped eating large meals after 5 p.m.– every day! I walked three miles three times a week, and I, drank eight glasses of water each day."

Based upon that simple vision and questioning exercise, you instantly know which habits are important to track and can modify the minimums and tracking periods over time based upon results!

The Habit Factor has also become popular for the simple fact that it distinguishes itself from the ubiquitous "Daily Task List" or "To-Do List," which nearly everyone lives by. Unfortunately, the challenge with To-Do lists is they are literally endless lists that capture all the noise in our daily lives: "call Bob," "transfer money," "feed the fish," "pick up apples," etc. Task lists are very helpful, but when it comes to achieving our goals they prove to be completely irrelevant.

Nomenclature of The Habit Factor® Methodology

As with the application of any skill, there tends to be an associated nomenclature that facilitates its practical application. In the case of The Habit Factor, it is evident that those who use the proper terminology understand the process better and realize better results.

This may sound rudimentary, but it is important to understand that "Goals" and "Habits" are really two distinctly different things. This distinction is vital as it sets up the foundation for the important relationship and alignment of supportive habits to any particular goal. Unfortunately, these two terms are commonly interchanged, and if you were to look across the spectrum of other habit and goal methodologies (and applications), you find in almost every case the two terms are confused.

Incorrect example: Goal "to write for 20 minutes." In the context of this system, that is *not* the goal. That is the supportive habit. The goal is to "write a book," and the *habit* is to "write for 20 minutes."

The terminology for "Goal" is also misused for what is labeled "**Target** *Minimums*" (per behavior) and "**Target** *Frequency*" (per week). The Target Minimum is the minimum success criteria (*identified by quantity or time*) established for each habit, such as, "Run for **20** minutes," or "do **50** pushups."

"Target Frequency" is the number of desired successful habits achieved in any one Tracking Period. The target frequency might be 18 days out of a Tracking Period that includes 30 days. Both the Target Frequency and Target Minimum should not be referred to as Goals. *Incorrect*

Example: "My goal is to perform this behavior/habit "18 days out of the next 30 days." Rather than labeling that as your Goal, it's better to refer to it as the Target Frequency. Again, the Goal is to "Write a Book," and in this case the Target Frequency is to "write for 20 minutes a day" 18 days over the next 30 days. This is an important distinction to make in order to become more accurate with the related nomenclature of goal achievement, and ultimately help you better achieve your true goals.

Quick Summary: To realize any goal, momentum is critical! With The Habit Factor, this can be quickly achieved by simply identifying 1-3 Key Habits (no more than five initially) that will help you reach your goal, and then TRACK them on a *daily* basis. That's it!

Frequently Asked Questions

1) I just want to create a new habit. I don't have a BIG goal or any goal at the moment.
Sure, you can skip the Goal Setup process and start the process at Step 6. Identify any habit you'd like to develop, establish its *minimum success criteria*, Target days (per week), and the Start and End Date for the Tracking period.

2) I don't want to have a Tracking Period. I want this habit for life.

In order to form a habit that ultimately requires no tracking, the idea is to track your actual performance of the habit vs. your ideal Target Frequency. If you elect to not have a Tracking period, you have no basis upon which to compare your actual behaviors vs. your ideals. Therefore, a tracking period is very important.

3) I want to quit smoking. Why shouldn't I track my negative habit?

If you track your negative habit, your attention and energy are directed toward the negative habit. As previously stated, a more effective way to eliminate a bad habit is to replace it with a positive one. In the case of smoking, for instance, perhaps "chewing gum" or "drinking water" becomes the positive habit that is tracked. Otherwise, you might set the Minimum Quantity to "0" for Smoking, and each day you achieve 0 instances of Smoking, you've been successful for the day.

4) Why do I see "Running 20 Minutes" as one of the *core* five habits if the goal is to write a book?

In a word, **balance**. Balance is *everything*. John Wooden believed balance, as a virtue, was second only to love. Be warned: There are some coaches who actually contend that "balance is bogus." The fallacy with this statement is it fails to appreciate *time* and the *dynamism of life*. Life exists only within the construct of time. Consider a tightrope walker: If you took a snapshot of her, she'd never appear in balance (at any particular moment in time). However, she remains perfectly balanced. This is because her adjustments are channeled throughout time. Similarly, when I coach people to align habits to their goal, I like to ensure that at least one core habit is related to health. (I prefer two: one diet and one exercise.) These healthy habits have a way of ensuring you feel good, maintain high energy and stay creative, all which help to accelerate the achievement of any goal! Balance can be thought of as a result, not a moment in time – you achieve balance. The Super Bowl winner each year is the most balanced team, with an effective offense comprised of a running and passing game. They have a top defense that likely creates a lot of turnovers. Their special teams play is outstanding, and finally, they have *chemistry* – largely a result of the aforementioned balance. *Seek balance with time.*

5) If I'm just tracking habits and "capturing time," how will I know *what* I should be doing next?
In the age of the Internet, lack of knowledge or information is rarely the issue. The common challenge is momentum, focus and execution. By **tracking** the behavior (habit), the enhanced awareness and focus tends to present the next steps. Chances are good there are several people who have achieved your goal and have shared the process; your challenge is to execute.

.

APPLICATION BACKGROUND

The following includes some real-life anecdotes as well as supportive documentation and important mindsets/beliefs (*thought habits*) essential to facilitate goal achievement. A few of these stories account for the formation of The Habit Factor methodology, and I also related a few notable episodes in working with others who have applied this system.

CATALINA CLASSIC: PART DEUX, MIND GAMES

In the Prologue I mentioned I'd revisit the Catalina Classic – a journey across an ocean channel that delivered far more than I'd bargained for. In hindsight, the undertaking helped me identify and forge some chief mindsets/beliefs (thought habits) that have served me well as I've pursued some other goals.

As mentioned, my goal was to paddle 32 miles, and initially I literally fell off the board having not made it 10 feet! After that first paddling experience, had I not already paid money to sign up for the event and purchased a new paddleboard, I would have given up. I can clearly recall being so excited to get my new board in the water, one that cost about $1,000, and yet I could barely even lie on it without falling off. Given that embarrassment and the fact that I was a complete disaster, I really wanted to quit.

Mindset #1: Quitting is *not* an option. Anyone can quit and *most people do*. Hence, few actually realize their goals.
Mindset #1a: From T. Harv Eker, "Every master was once a disaster."

I continued my training, and slowly my balance on the board became better. I found I could paddle about one-half mile without falling off the board. Then it was a mile, then three miles. The trick to long-distance paddling actually involves being able to shuffle your body from your chest to your knees, since lying on your chest for seven hours or more makes your rib cage feel like it's made of stone. Initially, this transition to my knees from lying on my chest proved impossible. I simply couldn't do it.

Mindset #2: Ben Franklin, "He that can have patience can have what he will."

My plan was to begin paddling three times a week, three miles each time. A couple of weeks into the process, I could finally see my progress. I was a long way from my goal, but I found enough confidence to sign up for a "short" seven-mile race. I ended up finishing – barely. The swell that day was huge and all the paddlers expended a lot of energy just to get to the *starting* line, which was just beyond the waves. In fact, a handful of people never made it to the starting line. For that race, I finished in nearly last place. I was mortified, embarrassed and most of all completely wiped out. I felt physically ill and emotionally crushed. Seven miles and it almost killed me, and now I had about four months to be ready for 32 miles. All available "data" suggested there was no way I was going to be able to make it come August 24.

Mindset #3: "Success is not final and failure is not fatal: It's the courage to continue that counts." ~Winston Churchill

At this point, I started doing something that was absolutely critical: I began tracking each training session. I logged the distance, the time and even commented in a notes section about the various related information. I kept notes on my relative strength during and after each workout, the conditions of the weather and the water, my weight and even my meal the night before. If I felt it was relevant, I noted it as part of the training and tracking process.

I ended up doing another shorter event about a month later and found that I moved up the pack a little. I understood the importance of celebrating progress, any progress, and managed to remain positive about the experience. Along the way, I visualized myself crossing the finish line of the Catalina Classic, although as things still were at that time, all "real" indications seemed to say there would be no way I could finish.

Mindset #4: "You have to believe it to see it."

This is the opposite of the cliché, "I'll believe it when I see it." When you set your goals you must believe they are possible first, and then you'll be able to envision the successful outcome. *Believe it to see it.*

Approximately two months before the Catalina event, there was a 20-mile race called the Bay to Bay. I recognized this as a critical milestone, since I believed if I could paddle 20 miles and then still have nearly two more months to train, I might actually be able to pull it off. The Bay to Bay is known for its difficulty and many of the Catalina paddlers use it as a "tune-up" race. Unlike the Catalina Classic, you don't have an escort boat to provide food or hydration along the way so, if you run out of food or drink, you will most likely not finish. I can recall being very concerned about hydration as I had no experience paddling that far, so the ability to stay hydrated yet conserve my water supply was just another aspect to the event I was forced to quickly learn.

While the Bay to Bay was by far the toughest event I'd endured up to that point, I completed it and I could finally see the months of training paying off. After all of the many mental and physical challenges, the 32 miles finally appeared within reason. My confidence grew too, as I noticed I moved up the pack of finishers again slightly. Each longer-distance event brought more experienced and faster paddlers, so I remained encouraged by the slightest progress.

So there you have it, four essential mindsets to foster the mental toughness necessary to tackle any goal. These are not just important – they are a requirement for anyone to achieve any goal, ever. It's impossible to achieve a worthwhile goal if you quit, aren't patient, do not persist or do not believe the goal is possible.

As I reflect on any past goal – the Ironman triathlons, or starting businesses, or even writing the book you're holding – all have required the very same, core mindsets (thought habits), and (like some sort of bonus gift) each challenge seems to lay a stronger foundation for future, bigger goals.

TWO SPHERES FOR ONE GOAL

When it comes to establishing habits, it's important to first recognize that effective change comes only by addressing both spheres of the human psyche: the conscious and the subconscious. Habit is the conduit.

Habits by definition are mindless acts, and this makes the conscious and deliberate development of a habit appear, at first, incongruous with its very nature (another paradox: mindfulness to produce a mindless, nearly effortless achievement). Once again, find the paradox and find the truth.

Since habits are deeply ingrained into your subconscious, they are extremely strong and often very difficult to break. A Chinese proverb underscores this point: "Habits are cobwebs at first and cables at last." Therefore, to be altered, they must be conscientiously addressed over time. Such diligence helps to drive new behaviors deep into the subconscious realm of habit.

Unfortunately, when attempting to change habits, most people address only the behavior on a conscious level. An example of this is dieting, which is a rational decision to modify your eating patterns. However, without the subconscious being involved or committed, the diet is set up for failure[22]. By involving the subconscious, emotional

---

[22] This is the reason we establish the "Why?" – to involve emotions that reside in the same place as habits: the subconscious.

brain in the decision to diet, the chances for success are increased since the food itself is rarely the issue.

Several weight-loss books and studies have identified that habits are triggered by environmental cues. Eating habits are no different and, unfortunately, since these triggers are unconscious they go unnoticed. Here's a quick example: Think for a few moments about buttered popcorn from a movie theater, or even a fresh-cut lemon. Chances are you'll notice your mouth watered without any conscious direction. These thoughts (energy) have the power to transform your body's physiology, its chemical reaction at a level far beyond consciousness. This is why traditional forms of dieting tend to fail. To be effective, they must alter the thought patterns that enabled the weight gain in the first place. And, until those thought patterns are changed, the poor eating habits will continue.

Aristotle famously pointed out, "We are what we repeatedly do. Excellence, then, is not an act, but a habit."

This is what this Application section is about: reaching the heights of excellence, via applied awareness of habit. So, whether your goal is to regain balance in your life, establish a new diet or exercise routine or even start a new business, the excellence required will not be derived through a haphazard approach of misdirected actions. Instead, the successful outcome can only be the product of deliberate, well-crafted and aligned habits, produced through diligent tracking.

AWARENESS AND FAITH

"He who looks outside dreams
and he who looks inside awakens."
~*Carl Jung*

By now, I'm hopeful that you have a very different prism through which to view your habits. Not only should you consider habits as good (really good), you should view them as a sort of magic carpet willing and able to take you to your desired destination. However, there is no "magic" per se; this sort of achievement can happen only via applied awareness – taking constant inventory of your existing habits of thought, spoken word and action. Applied awareness is a perpetual questioning of whether your current habits are getting you closer to your goals and desired lifestyle or further away. The effectiveness of your results will depend on how frequently you inventory and craft new habits and how often you set new goals.

Consciously crafted, repeated actions create habits that automatically direct you to a new desired destination, much like tweaking the autopilot settings on a plane. You change the settings, and therefore you alter the course and the destination. The plane won't just head in that direction for a minute; it's set on autopilot to remain in that direction, ultimately arriving at its desired destination nearly every time.

So, while this seems quite obvious, people frequently doubt the end result. This is like getting a few thousand feet in the air and a few miles toward your destination and then abruptly changing course. Such doubt is literally *fatal* to any successful arrival. In fact, success requires consistency of effort. You must be driven first by the belief that the achievement of the goal/destination is possible. With that repeated belief, a positive thought habit is formed. Without that belief, there is no incentive to maintain course and all likelihood of a successful outcome is essentially lost.

So, the most common breakdown, at least initially, is often a lack of belief and trust. People will change and often form new behaviors, or at least try to for a short period of time, but they eventually fail to establish a habit. This is what Napoleon Hill, out of sheer frustration, discovered: no consistency of applied behavior. He found this was largely due to people not "seeing" their goal being achieved; this created doubt and uncertainty. With doubt and uncertainty firmly planted in their minds, the people fell back into their old routines – their old habits – which were responsible for bringing them to where they were in the first place. Consider Napoleon Hill's comment regarding the matter, "Faith is the only agency through which the cosmic force of Infinite Intelligence can be harnessed and used by humanity." Please re-read that quote!

Abandoning halfway or a quarter-way or at any point of the change process because you can not envision the destination is like driving only halfway to work but, since you couldn't see the office, you turned around. See how that goes over with the boss. "Sorry boss, my goal really was to

get to the office today, but I just couldn't *see* my successful
arrival. I couldn't literally see the office, so I figured there
was no way I was ever going to make it. I just decided to
turn around and go home."

Before you ask, "Where does that faith and belief come
from?" recognize that it comes from the same place that
takes you confidently to the office, store or any other
physical destination you can't initially see, but somehow find
your way to. There is no difference. Similarly, abandoning
any destination (goal) after your initial outset makes about
the same sense. Remain convinced that the little actions, the
routine habits have set you on a course that makes it
possible to arrive at your goal every time.

MEET BENJAMIN FRANKLIN

*He was one of the most extraordinary
human beings the world has ever known. Born
into the family of a Boston candle maker,
Benjamin Franklin became the most famous
American of his time. He helped found a new
nation and defined the American character.
Writer, inventor, diplomat, businessman,
musician, scientist, humorist, civic leader,
international celebrity . . . genius.* [x]
~PBS.org

Coincidentally, at the time I started to design The Habit Factor mobile app, I pulled an old book off my shelf. Written by Frank Bettger, the book was titled, *How I Raised Myself from Failure to Success in Selling.* Bettger's final chapter in the book is, "Ben Franklin's Secret of Success and What It Did for Me." Here, he explained how he applied Ben Franklin's methodology for self-improvement and how it radically improved his own life. Bettger's reasoning was simple enough; he figured if one of the wisest men who ever lived thought the process of daily tracking his virtues was important, it certainly made sense for him to give it a try.

The story goes that a young Ben Franklin became very aware of his personality deficiencies; he was known to be a bit unrefined and was often argumentative. He reportedly recognized that the best path to reach his personal goals and ambitions was to refine his character. In order to do this, he identified the virtues that would most likely carry him forward to become successful. (By the way, this is a perfect example of aligning values with timeless principles.) The virtues he chose were: Temperance, Silence, Order, Resolution, Frugality, Industry, Sincerity, Justice, Moderation, Cleanliness, Tranquility, Chastity, and Humility.

When I came across Bettger's tale of his own experience practicing a variation of Ben's method, I found myself revisiting Ben's autobiography and, indeed, there it was! Ben penned in the last section, at the age of 79, that he attributed much of his life's success to the daily practice of tracking his virtues, one virtue a week. In fact, this is Ben's exact statement regarding the process of daily tracking: "I hope, therefore, that some of my descendants may follow the example and reap the benefit." Powerful stuff!

Dwell on that for a moment. This came from perhaps the most accomplished, renowned and influential American of all time. The process was relatively straightforward and simple. Essentially, Ben would track his single virtue each day for one week to measure his progress. He did this diligently. The specific method he used was to erase little tick marks next to the virtue based upon the incidents of infraction. After one week was over, he would then begin the process with the next virtue until he had tracked all 13.

He would then start all over. He did this repeatedly for years.

It was at this point I recognized the incredible similarities between his process for establishing virtues and mine for achieving goals. However, instead of tracking virtues (refined by habit), I was tracking supportive behaviors (developing habits) to achieve my goals.

ENTER THE MASTER-MIND

"No two minds ever come together without thereby creating a third — a third invisible, intangible force that may be likened to a third mind."
~Napoleon Hill

As pointed out earlier, the mind should be recognized as a metaphysical link, bridging our physical nature to that of the invisible and non-physical realms. The mind has proven essential to creativity and achievement, and when its energies are directed and concentrated in harmony with our intentions and goals, the accomplishments always prove astonishing. So, what happens when you combine multiple minds toward a singular purpose? Well, what you get is what Napoleon Hill termed "The Master-Mind."

Hill wrote in great detail about the Master Mind in
Think and Grow Rich. He defined the Master-Mind as an
alliance of like-minded persons who work in the spirit of
"harmony" (interesting given what we've noted earlier about
the importance of harmony). Nonetheless, it was Andrew
Carnegie who shared the Master-Mind concept with Hill,
suggesting that it was only through his own Master-Mind
alliance that he was able to achieve such extraordinary
results in business.

Having read Napoleon's account of the Master-Mind, I
considered joining a professional entrepreneurs group for
just this reason, believing that by joining forces with like-
minded peers I'd learn from their experiences and discover
best practices that would help our company. And, given that
I'd be able to help other members reach their goals, chances
were good they could help me reach mine.

About a year later, our company was looking for a new
building, the broker, who recognized I was an entrepreneur,
asked if I was familiar with a group called EO
(Entrepreneurs' Organization, www.eonetwork.org; YEO at
the time). He recommended that I look into it. Ultimately, I
ended up joining EO, and within it a forum called "The
Rock."

About two years into my EO and forum experience,
members of the Rock decided to collectively set goals –
BIG goals – and use each other for support, accountability
and even added peer pressure. At that time, I offered up
The Habit Factor methodology, which was responsible for
my achieving some fairly substantial goals and helping me
gain some badly needed balance in my life. Coincidently,

many of the members at the time were seeking "more balance" in their lives and expressed a keen interest in trying The Habit Factor.

I explained the process in detail to this successful group of entrepreneurs, and they unanimously agreed to give it a try. After the first 30 days (we met monthly), the response was overwhelmingly positive. One member said, "Besides the forum itself, this is the most valuable thing I've gotten from EO." Another called the process "magical." I was thrilled to see the process and success so quickly duplicated and the incredible momentum and excitement generated after only the first 30 days. The members of the group were already high achievers, so their use and feedback proved powerful! We naturally used 30-day tracking periods, and as the months progressed, we shared the results of our tracking for each important habit each time we met.

Members began to get fit, lose weight, increase sales, etc.; collectively, we were all moving closer to our goals simply by creating and tracking our key daily habits tied to our big goal.

See below for what The Habit Factor process looked like in the early days.

The Habit Factor® My Tracking Form (Early Days)

Note: In the early days, the Target day column had a "G" for Goal. That has since been changed to a "T" for Target, representing the Daily Target (1=Yes, 0=No). This also helps to distinguish the "real" goal from the Target day; this distinction was reviewed previously in the nomenclature section.

The example below is a personal form used in
December 2008. The five habits listed across the top in the
columns were: "Wake up before 8 a.m." (which later
evolved to "out of bed by 6:30 a.m.), "Write 1 Hr. on
THF," "Run 20 Minutes," "50 Pushups,"
"AdWords/Affiliates." At the time, each habit supported
multiple personal goals: "Write a Book," "Get Fit/Achieve
Balance" and "Increase Sales."

The example below is a partial form shared by a
member of our entrepreneurs group who set out to achieve
specific weight loss. See his "Notes" column, where he
would track his daily workouts and capture his daily weight
and progress.

	Habit Alignment Sheet						Excellence then, is not an act, but a HABIT. ~Aristotle
:b Mar Apr May 2009							

Work Out 30 - 45 Minutes		Non Alcohol Days		Weigh in and Monitor Blood		%	Comments:
G	A	G	A	G	A	%	
1	1	1	1	1	0.5		192lbs 124/85 69BPM Elliptical
1	1	1	1	1	1		191lbs 124/84 66BPM Weights
1	1	1	1	1	1		192lbs 125/85 61BPM Elliptical
1	1			1	1		192.6lbs 128/82 71BPM weights
	1	1		1	1		193lbs 129/88 95BPM Elliptical
	1	1		1	1		193.6lbs 136/83 105BPM Wakeboarded
4	6	6	4	7	6.5	94%	
		1	1	1	1		194.2lbs 132/83 84BPM
1	1	1	1	1	1		191lbs 119/79 63 BPM Elliptical
1	2	1	1	1	1		191.8 112/72 63BPM Weights & Elliptical
1	2	1	1	1	1		189.6lbs 119/71 78BPM Elliptical AM Wakeboar
	2	1	1	1	1		189.6lbs 105/66 63BPM Weights AM & Wakebo
				1	1		190.2lbs 115/63 66BPM
				1	1		191.4lbs 107/55 60 BPM
3	7	5	5	7	7	105%	
		1	1	1	1		192lbs 112/68 64 BPM
1	1	1	1	1	1		188.8lbs 118/60 66BPM Eliptical
1	1				1		188.6lbs 115/67 62BPM Wakeboarded

Note: The user was still getting familiar with the tracking process and initially gave himself multiple credits within one day; note the "2's". Proper tracking allows for only one check per day.

Today, most of our forum uses the app however the tracking form has been updated and is a bit more refined. I've provided a sample form with some partial data. (Again, you can find *free* templates at the sites mentioned at the top of this section.)

The Habit Factor®

PERIOD:

GOAL:

DAILY TARGET COLUMN! Targets for Week. 1= DO IT! 0=Non Target Day

Actuals Column: Did you do it? 1= YES!, 0=NO!

DAY		Habit #1 T	A	Habit #2 T	A	Habit #3 T	A	Habit #4 T	A	Habit #5 T	A	
Wednesd	13	1	0	1	1	1	1	1	0	1	0	
Thursday	14	1		0								
Friday	15	0		1								
Saturday	16	1										
Sun	17	0										Daily Comments:
Weekly SubTotal		3	0	2	1	1	1	1	0	1	0	25%
Monday	18	1	1	1	1	1	1	1	0	1	0	
Tuesday	19											
Wed	20											
Thursday	21											
Friday	22											
Saturday	23											
Sunday	24											
Weekly SubTotal		1	1	1	1	1	1	1	0	1	0	60%
Monday	25	1	1	1	1	1	1	1	1	1	0	
Tuesday	26											
Wed	27											
Thursday	28											
Friday	29											
Saturday	30											
Sunday	31											
Weekly SubTotal		1	1	1	1	1	1	1	1	1	0	80%

CASE STUDIES AND SETBACKS

While all members progressed toward their goals, results varied and a few ultimately did not achieve their goals. The information was telling and proved to be positive, as it helped us all to better understand the discriminating factors between those who realized their goals and those who did not.

Issue #1: The Goal changed.

It turns out that in at least one case, it appeared the "Why?" wasn't compelling enough and, in fact, the person ultimately decided that after moving toward his goal, it was not a goal he really wanted to achieve after all. He ultimately changed his goal.

Issue #2: Their habitat (environment) "sucked" them back into old routines and habits.

In one case, a participant who made stunning progress in the first couple of months and lost nearly all the desired goal weight fell back into his old habits. As the months progressed he acknowledged being sucked back into certain behaviors, relationships and environments that were unsupportive to his new behaviors. When combined with his decreasing commitment to track his new behaviors, his environments and old habits proved too strong. Here was a perfect example where his willingness and commitment needed to be greater than the force of his environments. This example demonstrated that with greater awareness of his habitat, he could have tracked associated environmental habits and been able to mitigate those negative associations responsible for sparking his bad dietary decisions and habits.

Issue #3: Circumstances arose and weakened belief.

Another member simply didn't *believe* he was capable of achieving the stated goal: He didn't feel ready to attempt a triathlon on a specified date. I shared with him that I personally believed he could have achieved his goal, but as Henry Ford pointed out, "Whether you think you can or you can't, you are correct."

Regardless, his experience altered his diet and exercise habits. Today he's far better for making the attempt. He has also now reset a new physical goal, and I'm confident that, given his belief and commitment do not waiver, the process will help him achieve his new goal!

Bottom Line / Summary:

In each instance, the methodology itself proved effective and also demonstrated that there are underlying mindsets/beliefs (habits) related to the ultimate formation of any habit that effect the goal's outcome. These "failures" proved as important as the successes, since they provide significant information for anyone planning to achieve their goals.

WHAT GETS YOU THERE UNFORTUNATELY OFTEN KEEPS YOU THERE

It's another great paradox of habit: The same habits that might at one point help you achieve great heights, later prove limiting and make you feel as though you're in a rut. Habits serve us until the comfort they provide becomes too great and inhibit growth.

It's a good idea to view your habits (good ones and bad ones) as though they were planets orbiting around the sun. Some habits are undoubtedly larger, more influential and likely to have far greater *gravitational* pull than others. The benefit, of course, is once a habit is within the grasp of a strong enough gravitational pull, its orbit becomes automated – the habit is engaged.

Based on Kepler's three laws of planetary motion, Newton formulated his own elegant and concise theory about how these empirical laws might be derived from ideas relating to the universal attraction of matter. Newton developed his theories of gravitation in 1666 (at 23 years old). In 1686, he presented the three laws of motion, which, upon further review, share some unmistakable parallels to habits.

Newton's first law: *Every object will remain at rest or in uniform motion in a straight line unless compelled to change its state by the action of an external force. This is normally taken as the definition of inertia.*

The second law: *The velocity of an object changes when it is subjected to an external force.*

The third law: *For every action (force) in nature, there is an equal and opposite reaction.*

The key point of Newton's first two laws is that if there is no net force acting on an object, the object will maintain a constant velocity and direction. Think about this object in motion as our habits and, in turn, the direction in which they take our lives. If we do not actively change or direct our habits, they will simply repeat themselves until a force greater than them finally compels them to change.

For better or worse, everyone develops natural patterns of habitual thought, channels through which our minds run all too easily, resulting in recurring conditions. In fact, it's so natural to assume these habits that they've become *obfuscated*, nearly inseparable from life itself. This may help explain why habit, as a subject matter, has yet to become a major study within our educational institutions.

CHOICE: THE ULTIMATE FREEDOM

"While we are free to choose our actions, we are
not free to choose the consequences of our actions."
~Stephen R. Covey

The excellent stock trader wakes up earlier, researches more, and is a product of his successful habits (directed toward his goals). The outstanding executive also wakes up earlier, schedules her time effectively and finds ways to constantly feed her mind to learn and grow. Both perform these actions as daily habits conceived originally by choice. And both examples prove the adage: Show me a successful person in any endeavor and I'll show you a person with superior and supportive, positive habits. Brian Tracy shares it this way: "Successful people simply have 'success habits.'"

"Man becomes what he thinks about all day long," said Emerson, and countless other great thinkers concur. So, it should be of little surprise that it is our habitual thinking that is responsible for this "becoming."

However, with proper awareness and conscientious choice, we can select and refine our thoughts to construct our own "success" habits and thereby create our own ideal future.

The *very* first power of choice is to guide our personal energies – choice directs our life, being and character. Recall the sailing metaphor: If habit is analogous to the powerful

force of the wind and carries us to our destination, then
what is our tiller? That is, what steers and directs us toward
our destination/our destiny?

Correct. Choice.

With our individual freedom to choose, we decide from
one moment to the next whether we should drive our minds
to the garbage dump or to greener pastures, to sail toward
calm seas or into dramatic and rough waters. And, just as
our habits accumulate and compound, so too do our
choices. Or, to be more accurate, it is our choices'
consequences that compound. Each seemingly inconsequential
decision influences the next, and so on.

If you recall our previous discussion of paradox and
truth, then you ought to find this interesting. The choice of
discipline and diligence actually produces freedom, whereas
the avoidance of discipline and diligence (in pursuit of
freedom) produces a form of personal imprisonment. Let
me clarify.

When you choose discipline, you lay the foundation for
freedom. Zig Ziglar has a wonderful quote for this: *"If you do
the things you ought to do, when you ought to do them, the day will
come when you can do the things you want to do, when you want to do
them."*

By avoiding hard work and discipline, people forge the
habit of laziness or, as Ben Franklin labeled it, "sloth," and
cling to a false sense of contentment that ultimately catches
up to them. Here's what Ben Franklin has to say about
diligence and industry in his book, *The Way to Wealth*:

"Diligence is the mother of good luck. God gives all things to industry. Then plough deep, while sluggards sleep, and you shall have corn to sell and to keep. Work while it is called today, for you know not how much you may be hindered tomorrow. One today is worth two tomorrows.

Interestingly, in his book *Outliers*, Mr. Gladwell identifies *one constant* among *all* of his success case studies. He calls it the "10,000 hour rule," perhaps yet another way to call attention to The Habit Factor[xi]. In this case, he refers to the *habit* of discipline – the habit of industry and diligence. So, as he explained, whether it was the Beatles playing night after night for years, refining their performances, or a young Bill Gates investing thousands of hours into his computer programming skills, all great achievers don't just work harder; they work "much, much harder." This is what the 10,000-hour rule represents: a minimum of ten thousand hours of work refining one's skills and related fundamentals through practice. So, when you overlay the 10,000-hour rule on top of The Habit Factor's theory that habit is a language facilitating creativity, you can see exactly why the 10,000-hour rule demonstrates such consistency.

While chance is an element that nobody can seem to control, working harder and developing an established *work ethic that becomes a habit* is within everyone's control.

Michelangelo, the great Italian Renaissance artist, summarized both his skill and success rather judiciously: "If people knew how hard I worked to get my mastery, it wouldn't seem so wonderful after all."

So, back to choice: But, you ask, what about the sailor who elects to direct his energies fruitfully and chooses to sail to calm waters but is overcome by an unexpected and horrific storm?

Well, even in the direst of circumstances – figurative or literal – we retain the power and freedom of choice! Therefore, conscientious choice ought to be regarded as your most prized asset since, with mastery, it can literally provide mental peace of mind and freedom even when, in the physical sense, neither exists.

Dr. Viktor Frankl shared this very personal and profound insight in his classic best-seller, *Man's Search For Meaning*, Frankl, having suffered more than two-and-a-half years in Nazi concentration camps, came to realize that even in the worst of conditions, dictated by circumstances far beyond his control, *he still retained the freedom to choose his thoughts.* He concluded that such thought control was a form of personal liberty and regardless of circumstance could never be taken away.

Even though he was physically abducted and his wife and mother were ultimately murdered by the Nazis, Frankl somehow managed to recognize the remarkable capacity to *choose meaning* to his unimaginable situation. He chose to channel his limited energy to a vision of survival. For survival meant he would later share the horrors of what he endured to ensure future generations would never experience such atrocities again.

So, while we may never understand the random and tragic events that severely impact our lives, we always retain the freedom and ability to choose our response. With this freedom, we can assign any meaning to any event or misfortune. It's this type of elevated, conscientious choice that tends to go beyond serving just one individual and so often, ultimately, serves an even greater cause. Consider any charity; whether it is MADD, Make-A-Wish, or Big Brothers Big Sisters of America, and you're likely to find tragedy redefined through conscientious choice to serve the greater good.

On a personal level, I believe mastery of thought, ultimately, is responsible for our happiness.

How?

Recall from the introduction Buddha's powerful statement, "There is no way to happiness. Happiness is the way." Indeed. *Happiness is a choice.*

In fact, when you consider all the typical personality success traits, they all prove to originate, at first, from choice. For instance, enthusiasm is a choice, as is motivation, love, persistence, focus, responsibility, honesty, integrity, courage, etc. All of these "success" traits must be born from choice and then refined by habit to become a virtue. This, of course, is the same epiphany Ben Franklin had as a young man when he decided to track his 13 virtues.

Now, let's consider Aristotle's earlier observation, that virtue is crafted only through habit, and you can see we've come full circle. The process or flow diagram, if you will, for personal development and character refinement looks something like this:

Awareness ➔ *Choice* ➔ *Action (if repeated)* ➔ *Habit* = *Virtue*

Awareness is necessary; choice sparks the awareness (thought energy) for action. Repeated action forms the habit, and habit results in virtue. Everything about our character is crafted through habit. Recall one of the definitions of habit: "An established disposition of the Mind or Character."

Habit is character, and character is habit.

You may be familiar with the often-quoted anonymous motivational saying that begins, "Watch your thoughts, for they become words. Watch your words, for they become actions…" etc. Well, as powerful as that message is, I've always had a slight fundamental issue with it. While awareness is critical (the "watch" part of that quote), it is conscientious *choice* that sets the energy in motion – meaning watching is one thing and choosing is another. So, given that we are exposing/unleashing/examining the power of choice, I'd like to share a slightly different version of that famous motivational quote. The Habit Factor's version:

Choose your thoughts, for they become words.
Choose your words, for they become actions.
Choose your actions, for they become habits.
Choose your habits, for they become character.
Choose your character, and it becomes your destiny.

THE ONLY GUARANTEED WAY TO FAIL

At the beginning of the Application section, I asked if you've given much thought to what failure truly is. Unfortunately, it's a terrifying concept that prevents so many of us from ever getting started on any goal in the first place.

So, what is failure – really?

I'd like to share a quick story about how I came upon its real definition. I'll never forget the day. I had just posed that very question to a classroom of high school students. It was my fourth year of volunteer teaching for Junior Achievement (www.ja.org). The class I was teaching was titled "Success Skills," and the curriculum was part of a larger program entitled C.L.A.S.S.: Corporate Leaders Advocating Success Skills. As part of my volunteer effort, I really wanted to visit the most impoverished high schools within our county and share my personal experiences and some of these important life lessons with the students. I wanted to do my small part to inspire them and make sure they continued to believe in their abilities to realize their dreams. Each course I taught was 10 weeks long and each class was about one hour.

So, there I stood before the class. "What is failure?" I asked.

Since this was a course about "success skills," we not only had to define "success," I thought it was important to define failure as well, which unfortunately was absent from the curriculum. Note: I modified the course's success definition only slightly, since its original definition was "Creating your future." That didn't sit too well with me, since I theorized you could live in a garbage can and still be creating your future. (I guess it did work for Oscar the Grouch). So, I decided that if we simply insert the word "ideal" between "your" and "future," it produced a fairly good, working definition for success. As in, "Success is creating your *ideal* future." Again, the word ideal demands your creative faculties, which are unique and absolutely necessary for personal achievement.

There we were, left to dwell upon that question and its possible answer (myself included). We knew that failure could not be the opposite of success. If anything, *failure has proven itself to be a prerequisite for success*, as a simple analysis of any great, successful person reveals countless "failures" along their journey. So, whether we considered Edison and, in his own words his "10,000 failures" while inventing the light bulb, or Abraham Lincoln and his long list of "failures" early in his career as a businessman and then politician (he lost several bids for Senate and Congress), it was agreed – *failure was not the opposite of success.*

I then asked for a show of hands to see if any student might have an answer. Only a few hands went up and there, in the front row, a beautiful Hispanic girl (I wish I could recall her name) raised her hand knowingly. I called upon her, and she stated with conviction, "Hopelessness!"

I almost fell over.

"Wow!" I thought. "Incredible!" There it was. The only sure way to fail – ever – is to be hopeless. For without hope there is no drive to proceed, no will to succeed. Without hope there is no energy, no willingness to march forward. Without hope, simply put, nobody stands a chance, *ever!*

So, let it be known, you are encouraged to remain hopeful whatever the cost. Regardless of the setback or "failure" *that is certain to come your way*, please recognize any failure for what it truly is – nothing other than feedback (energy) guiding you to redirect your energy and to press on! Always remain hopeful. Always press on! Recall what the great 30th president of the United States of America had to say on the subject of persistence, a trait that can exist only in the presence of hopefulness.

"Nothing in the world can take the place of persistence. Talent will not; nothing is more common than unsuccessful men with talent. Genius will not; unrewarded genius is almost a proverb. Education will not; the world is full of educated derelicts. Persistence and determination alone are omnipotent. The slogan 'Press On!' has solved and always will solve the problems of the human race."
~Calvin Coolidge

PROVIDENCE MOVES TOO

In the previously outlined goal-development process, we established that an essential ingredient to clarifying your goal is to emotionalize it via total commitment. Without total commitment, regardless of the process, you won't succeed. Obviously, the best goal process in the world will not help a person who is not committed to seeing his goal through. Abraham Lincoln once said, "Always bear in mind that your own resolution to succeed is more important than anything else."

One reason I believe commitment is such a determining ingredient is what I like to call the *frequency factor*. This is not the frequency factor noted in chemistry (chemical kinetics, which, interestingly, includes investigations of how different experimental conditions can influence *the speed of a chemical reaction*). But if you translate chemical reaction for physical reaction as it relates to the manifestation of a goal, you may see some interesting parallels.

As theorized earlier, the mind is at least in part comprised of the corresponding and related electromagnetic frequencies between the heart (measured by EKG) and the brain (measured by EEG). The theory is that when you completely *commit* to a goal and *emotionalize* it, its energy becomes amplified. When you combine that amplified energy with consistent thoughts and behaviors (habits) that are supportive of your intentions, you produce a signal that Infinite Intelligence not only receives, but I believe understands and facilitates.

While I'm sure this may sound a little cryptic, I can only cite the numerous instances of people who recognize that the achievement of their goal was only possible once a seemingly infinite array of events unfolded and coordinated with perfect precision. Please do not take my word on this, though; consider Johann Wolfgang Von Goethe, thought by many to be one of the most important and influential thinkers of Western culture. Here is what he had to say about commitment and synchronicity.

"The moment one definitely commits oneself, then providence moves too. All sorts of things occur to help one that would never otherwise have occurred. A whole stream of events issues from the decision, raising in one's favor all manner of unforeseen incidents and meetings and material assistance, which no man could have dreamed would have come his way."

The following is an account of one of the most recent and remarkable examples of synchronicity I've been witness to.

Meet Jon, an impressive entrepreneur in his own right who briefly "retired" at the age of 29 after selling an Internet-based company. Jon is a great friend and enlisted me (based upon my prior lifeguarding and big-wave surfing experience) to help him achieve a life-long dream of surfing the biggest wave of his life – a 30-foot wave into which I would tow him in on a Jet Ski. His goal was very *clear*, and he was totally *committed*. In fact, he was committed to the tune of about $20,000 or more.

In order to surf this dream wave we both trained for well over a year, practicing a form of surfing known as tow-in surfing. The idea is that when the waves become huge, your best bet to ride them effectively is to match their speed and force with that of a Jet Ski, which can tow you into the wave at high speed.

While the training itself required no particular "outside" assistance, when the fateful day arrived, February 14, 2010, a seemingly endless array of events unfolded, well beyond our sphere of influence. For starters, the swell itself had to be 30-feet-plus, and swells like that come through only about six times a year (at best). This was by far the largest swell of the year.

Then, the variable of our schedules came into play. We would both need to be healthy, ready and available when the swell hit. Previously, during the year either Jon or I would miss a fleeting opportunity to catch a swell due to scheduling conflicts. Jon tends to travel a lot and I have a number of commitments, so it began to appear that the chance of us catching such a swell when it worked with both our schedules was nearly impossible.

However, as fate would have it, when the largest swell of the year arrived on the weekend of February 14, we were both in town and (given my wife's remarkable capacity for generosity – it was Valentine's Day), we drove into Baja, Mexico filled with mixed emotions of fear and excitement.

The destination was "Killers" on Todos Santos Island, known within the surf community as one of the world's premiere big-wave spots. The next hurdle we anticipated would be crowds. Since we had a perfect swell (maybe too perfect), and were both available to attempt this questionable mission of sanity, we expected to have very limited access to the waves. We anticipated seeing a large number of professional surfers taking all the waves. "Well," I comforted Jon on the drive down, "at the very least, we'll get to witness the pros surfing these insane waves firsthand." This will be its own learning experience, I thought. Best-case scenario, we thought, we'd be left with the "smaller" waves – the scraps.

After a bumpy eight-mile Jet Ski ride to the tiny island in the early morning hours, we arrived and were shocked to see complete emptiness. There wasn't a surfer around. It was eerie, and the surf was huge. No Jet Skis and no other surfers; nothing but enormous waves crashing against the rocks. It was unfathomable! "What was going on?" we both wondered. Then, it occurred to us; there was a big-wave contest being held in Northern California the day before at a surf spot called Mavericks. This annual event pays $50,000 to the winner and lures all the top pros up the coast. We then theorized that all the non-pros were either too smart or too scared and decided to stay away from Killers.

So there we were, Jon and I, alone eight miles out at sea, sitting just off this tiny island watching the waves slam into the rocks. We sat on the Jet Ski and contemplated our next move. It was at that moment I couldn't help but think, "Be careful what you wish for."

The impossible had happened. We were alone, at one of the best big-wave spots on the planet with the biggest swell of the year and no other surfers in sight. We just sat there in total awe. Jon turned to me and nervously asked, "So, what do you think we should do?" I think he was hoping I might suggest we turn around and go back. All I could offer was a pretty feeble, "Let's just hang out and keep watching." My hope was to see if we could get any sense of rhythm from the sets and to see if, hopefully, some other surfers might show up.

Next thing we knew, another Jet Ski arrived and two surfers who were obvious big-wave veterans of the spot went straight into action. It was incredible: These guys were towing each other into waves bigger than anything either of us had ever witnessed firsthand. We continued to watch them and then realized the opportunity that lay before us. We decided it was time. Jon jumped into the water, and within less than a minute I was pulling him into a huge wave that was growing enormous underneath him. He was speeding down the face of the biggest, most powerful wave of his life. I rode alongside on the Jet Ski ready to swoop in if he fell. He rode the wave perfectly and came off the shoulder when his ride was finished. He was beaming – grinning from ear to ear. I hollered, "You did it! That was it! You nailed it! You hit your goal on the very first wave!"

It turned out to be one of the most magical days, and Jon and I traded waves with the other two surfers for nearly four hours. Exhausted, we realized it was better to quit while we were ahead, and still alive, able to share the experience[23].

---

[23] Check out Jon's blog for his blow-by-blow personal account at: http://joncarder.com/post/390105908/surf-a-30-foot-wave-before-i-die-check.

The Application, Precepts
(Ideas and Principles for Action)
<u>Ideas</u>

- Goals are not optional.
- The quickest way to establish momentum toward any goal is to establish and track its core, related habits.
- Habit alignment has been ignored as it relates to goal achievement.
- The SMART goal system fails to acknowledge habit alignment.
- Creativity is your essence and a requirement for goal achievement.
- Goals are metaphysical super-glue bonding you to your creative essence and your birthright to create your ideal future.
- *"You can't waste time, you can only waste yourself,"* George Mathew Adams
- *"The goal of life is full development of all your potential."* Jim Rohn
- Identify meaningful goals by writing your ideal obituary.
- To achieve any goal requires the involvement of both spheres of the human psyche: the subconscious and the conscious.
- Energy flows throughout the body to create emotional and physiological reactions essential to goal achievement.
- Apply awareness via questions to identify if your habits are getting you closer to your goals or further away.
- Faith is required to tap into the cosmic force of Infinite Intelligence.
- **Failure cannot exist where there is hope**.
- Habit alignment of thoughts and actions creates harmony of intentions. This helps to amplify and communicate clearly to Infinite Intelligence.
- Seek balance in all affairs. Balance is about constant adjustments, it is a result, not a moment in time.
- Be careful what you wish for.
- "It takes as much *energy* to wish as it does to plan." ~Eleanor Roosevelt.

Actions!

∞ On a scale of 1-10 (10 being best), rate the level of harmony in the following aspects of your life.

Primary relationship: _____

Work: _____

Family: _____

∞ Be like Roz. Write two versions of your obituary, one as though nothing changes, and the other as your *ideal* obituary.

∞ What major goal are you currently pursuing?

∞ What three habits would you need to develop or strengthen to achieve this goal?

IMPACT: APPLICATION PLUS:
P.A.R.R., Q & A, COACHING + EXTRAS

IMPACT

noun: impact; plural noun: impacts
ˈimˌpakt/

1. come into forcible contact with
another object.

"the shell impacted twenty yards
away"

2. *have a strong effect on someone or
something.*

---

*"To Think Is Easy. To Act Is Difficult. To
Act As One Thinks Is The Most Difficult."*
~Johann Wolfgang Von Goeth

P.A.R.R.: HABIT DEVELOPMENT SIMPLIFIED
(PLAN, ACT, RECORD & REASSESS)

A simple and foolproof method to intentionally craft habits supportive of your most important goals.

> *"The chains of habit are too weak to be felt until they are too strong to be broken."*
> ~Samuel Johnson

A key idea to introduce when it comes to habit development is HabitStrength™. Habit Strength (with a space) was originally introduced by influential psychologist Clark L. Hull (May 24, 1884–May 10, 1952), who coined this phrase based upon the idea that certain criteria (stimulus, response, drive, incentive, connectedness, etc.) all combine to influence the strength of any particular behavior/habit.[24]

HabitStrength™ as it relates to The Habit Factor and its P.A.R.R. methodology, is very similar in concept, but far less complex. Using weightlifting as a metaphor, HabitStrength assures us that any behavior/habit – with

---

[24] http://en.wikipedia.org/wiki/Clark_L._Hull

continued use and with increased repetition and frequency – *over time will become stronger.*

P.A.R.R. assures participants that when they **P**lan, **A**ct, **R**ecord (tracking + notes) and **R**eassess their habits, those habits will be strengthened over time. Ideally, those habits will be strengthened to a point where they no longer need to be tracked. This is essentially when one aspect of The Habit Factor kicks in, *automaticity*!

HabitStrength, related to P.A.R.R., is purely a derivative of what the participant (You) *can* control: intention (*Planning*), performance (*Acting*), tracking plus notes (*Recording*), and (*Reassessment*).

Each behavior (habit) is reassessed for its development (targets vs. actuals) after a 28-day period (four weeks). After 28 days, the participant has enough tracking data to assess whether their actual performance met set targets. This data also provides the participant with a real gauge of his or her commitment level to crafting the habit.

If, after 28 days, performance (actual vs. target) is above 85% for any particular habit, a participant is encouraged to "raise the bar" or "increase the weights" (metaphorically speaking).

For instance, a participant who wants to develop a reading habit may initially set a low target of reading 15 minutes a day, three times a week for the first 28 days. After the initial period of four weeks, with success (performance of 85% or above) she would then increase her targets to 25 minutes a day and four times a week.

If, however, she finds that she is below the target of 85% after her first four weeks, it is recommended that she continue another 28 days with <u>the same set of original</u> <u>targets</u> to see if she can improve her tracking score.

If she can't seem to reach her initial, "low bar" target of 85% for the behavior, she essentially has two options: determine if there is a real desire to develop the habit at all, or lower the bar a little ("reduce the weights") and begin again. This underscores why setting the initial target for each new habit very low helps to spur momentum and reinforce the feeling of success which is essential to the process.

There are many parallels to weightlifting with the habit-development process. For instance, anyone who might start to bench press for the first time isn't likely to start with 300 pounds. Yet any weightlifter will tell you that after about a month (if not sooner), the weights and frequencies originally set as targets will have become too easy and that to continue to increase strength, the weights and frequencies must be increased.

Note: The same number of repetitions or frequency per week is likely to yield different habit-development results per individual. Similar again to weight lifting: If I curl 35 pounds and you curl 35 pounds, we may have differing results based upon where we were when we started with regard to our skill, desire, etc.

SIX-MONTH JUMP-START THF COACHING PROCESS

"A problem well stated is a problem half solved."

~ *Charles F. Kettering*

Answer the following questions. For readers using an ebook, Kindle, iBook or audio format, you can download worksheet templates of these pages to fill out as needed. Please visit: http://thehabitfactor.com/templates.

Ask yourself the following questions:

1. In the next six months (or 9 or 12[25]), I'd like to achieve (be, do, have) the following (goal detailed below):

_____Example:___Marathon_____

_____$5K month passive income_____

_____

Estimated completion/achievement date: _____

_____

[25] This is great for 5- and 10-year periods as well. Recall that people tend to overestimate what they can accomplish in the short term and grossly underestimate what they can do in the long run!

It's worth recalling that the Latin root of the word "habit" equates to your *character* and/or present *condition*. Therefore, when a person says they want to achieve something, the implication is that they must first "be" something different and do something different – different habits. The late, great Zig Ziglar used to say, "You have to BE before you can DO and DO before you can HAVE!"

2. Now, imagine that it is six months later and you have achieved your goal. Dwell upon that thought. Congratulations! Can you visualize this accomplishment clearly? In fact, can you *feel* the emotions of what it's like to have achieved the goal? *(Visualize it now!)*

Most goal-achievement processes, such as the S.M.A.R.T. goals method, ask you to identify what you need to do to next – what next "steps" you should take.

Instead, we're going to do something much more effective and simple. Ask yourself, "What habits did I *have* (what recurring behaviors were created) that helped me achieve this goal?" The idea is to simply reflect on the habits that helped you achieve your goal – looking backward![26]

---

[26] Note: If you cannot see or feel the successful completion of the goal, consider revising the goal until it is believable (and you are able to visualize it). Example: modify a full marathon to a half, or go from making $10K/month in passive income to $2K/month as a starting point.

(Goal name) _____ *?*

3. What habits helped you complete your goal?

(Reflecting) The habits I created to support my above goal were:

1) _____
2) _____
3) _____
4) _____
5) _____

In essence, I became (*ex: more fit, a better writer*) _____ because I habitually (*ex: ran, wrote*) _____ and _____ and _____ and _____ and _____ .

    Back to Zig's model: You must BE someone different to DO things differently and HAVE achieved something different.

    In this successful scenario, it's important to recognize that over time you would have elevated the frequency of these habits per week as well as the "minimum success criteria" (per habit instance, recall the P.A.R.R. method in the previous section).

Using the marathon as an example, your running frequency would be much greater closer to the marathon than when you started training months earlier, when perhaps you ran for the first time – for example four or five times a week vs. just two. Also, the amount of time per run (minimum success criteria) would be much longer closer to the event, say 12 minutes vs. 45 minutes.

You may think there are some other habits required to achieve your goal. If that is the case (typically five and no more than seven habits will suffice for greatest effectiveness), you are encouraged to list all the habits you think you will need and then prioritize them by asking the following question.

4. Which single habit, if developed (through diligent tracking using the P.A.R.R. method), will have the greatest impact on my results/ability to achieve my goal?

This is an essential question because nearly everyone immediately knows the answer, and often this habit will be the most demanding to develop in terms of time and intensity. This habit should also be your main focus and priority. You should spend the most time determining the effective minimum success criteria and frequencies for both starting and what the ideal end-tracking period will look like. For example, when I began to write this book, for my initial tracking period I used targets of 20 minutes, 3 times a week.

Nearing the end, under deadline pressure and with my HabitStrength having improved over months of tracking, my target per day was as high as 90 minutes and the frequency was 5 times per week (these were minimums!).

Since tracking these behaviors is critical, understanding how to <u>limit tracking to the essential five habits</u> at the beginning is vital!

DO NOT BE TEMPTED TO INCREASE THE NUMBER OF HABITS YOU ARE ACTIVELY TRACKING.

A user wrote to our app-support desk because of her "speed" issue, and it was revealed to us that she was tracking 49 active habits!

If you list all the habits required and then prioritize them based upon the above question, you will quickly and easily identify the top five habits you should track to get the results you desire and, most importantly, you will know the most vital behavior responsible for the greatest impact!

Also, regard EVERYTHING as positive feedback. In other words, if you're not hitting your targets, it's OK; lower them or examine your desire level. If you realize you should be tracking other habits, that's wonderful. This is information you wouldn't have gathered had you not started the process of tracking something in the first place.

FREQUENTLY ASKED QUESTIONS HABITS, GOALS, MOTIVATION, WILLPOWER AND MORE

The majority of these topics have been addressed throughout various sections of this book; however, in the interest of consolidating the subject matter for quick reference, we've added this FAQ.

1) **How long does it take to form a habit? I've heard it takes 21 days.**
   The short answer is habit formation varies greatly. There are a multitude of factors influencing the formation of any habit, including the difficulty of the behavior, knowledge, desire, skill, willingness, and many other psychological factors. Therefore, for one person it may take 19 days to develop a "flossing habit," and yet for another it may take 72 days or more. Please revisit the "Scientific Section" and "21-Day Habit Theory" earlier in the book.

2) **Do you have to enjoy a habit for it to stick?**
   Well, last time I checked there were plenty of women who put on makeup habitually who don't enjoy it. I can pretty much shave without much conscious thought as

well as tie my necktie, yet I'm not a big fan of either. I even maintain the habit of shaving (most of the time). Sadly, this is another Internet-propagated fallacy about habit. Interestingly, it reminds me of the great observation by Ed Foreman that the difference between successful people and unsuccessful people can be found in their habits. He would go on to say, "Successful people do the things that the unsuccessful people do not want to do, like get up early, work hard, stay late, work out, etc. Only the 'funny' thing is, the successful people don't like doing those things either, but they do them anyway!"

Now, having said all that, there is no doubt that enjoyment *helps* to foster and maintain a habit, but it's not a requirement.

3) **How come I have so many bad habits, but I never had to track any of them in order to create them?**
Humans have been described as creatures of habit, and it's for a good reason: We are developing habits all the time. As energy beings, we are wired to consciously and/or subconsciously record and repeat those experiences that proved valuable or, on some level, intrinsically rewarding. This reminds me of a Phillip B. Crosby saying: "Good things only happen when planned; bad things happen on their own." More often than not, the same can be said for habit. Habit, by design, makes these repeated efforts more efficient over time. Animals come pre-wired with instincts. Humans are totally unique in their capacity to intentionally craft

habits that serve their desires and goals. Animals have essentially two basic goals: self-preservation and reproduction. Therefore, their habits or instincts come "pre-packaged" to help them achieve those goals in the most efficient way possible. This may sound a bit paradoxical, but when you are able to become extremely aware and conscious of your unconscious behaviors, you have the ability to direct and craft new unconscious behaviors (habits) consciously to serve your goals, desires and ambitions.

4) **What if I miss a day tracking my habit? Will that hurt my chances of forming a habit?**
   NO. In fact, this is why The Habit Factor introduced the concept of "target" days for habit development. You can intend to perform a behavior on Monday, Wednesday or Friday (for instance), and still develop the habit. Originally, I only had anecdotal evidence of this from my own experiences and coaching others; however, the truth has been validated in this study,[27] which essentially demonstrates that habit development is based upon consistency over time and is not impacted by a missed day here or there.

---

[27] Lally, P., van Jaarsveld, C., Potts, H., and Wardle, J. (2010). How are habits formed: Modelling habit formation in the real world. European Journal of Social Psychology.

5) **What about the requirement for a "treat" or a "reward" to develop a habit?**
There is no requirement for a "reward" in order to develop a habit – another unfortunate myth. Rewards, particularly in the form of something extrinsic like a piece of cake, are not required to develop a habit. This theory really derives from studies with rats (largely), whose behavior can be altered and measured with extrinsic rewards. Note: That same study mentioned previously (footnote below) confirms that "rewards" had been given way too much credit for habit formation. The last thing I need to do is eat a piece of cake after I've performed my "running" habit. <u>One of the greatest *intrinsic* rewards is the self-efficacy of performing the behavior as Planned and Recording /(tracking) it.</u> Therefore, the act of tracking might be considered its own great reward, and at the same time helps to reaffirm the habits development.

6) **I've heard that some habits can be more important than others. Is that true?**
Since habits are often the result of triggers or cues that, in fact, can be other habits, there are a handful of habits that are considered foundational or "keystone," thereby influencing other behaviors/habits. For instance, "getting out of bed early" is associated with increased productivity, better scheduling, a healthier outlook, etc. The habit of "running" may trigger other supportive, positive habits, including a better diet. You won't find

too many chain smokers who are habitual runners.

7) **What are some of the more powerful keystone/foundational habits?**

From my experience, developing a positive mindset/ positive disposition (thought habits) is very foundational – and may be one of the hardest habits to develop. Physical fitness, working out/running would be another powerful keystone habit. Becoming a habitual goal-setter sets forth a whole series of supportive, positive habits. Getting out of bed early is likely the world's greatest productivity "secret" and also springs forth many other positive habits.

8) **How do you create "thought habits," such as being positive or even enhancing mindfulness?**

Dandapandi, a Hindu spiritualist[28] (former monk, now interestingly enough on an entrepreneurial speaking circuit), spoke to our entrepreneur group (EO) specifically about how to develop "consistent practices" (you and I might know these "consistent practices" as "habits"). It seemed he too was a bit confined by the negative connotation of the word. In fact, I don't think I heard him say "habit" once in nearly four hours. I could hardly wait to see his method to develop a "consistent practice." I was literally sitting on the edge

---

[28] http://www.thehabitfactor.com/2014/03/to-develop-mindfulness-you-must-first-develop-the-corresponding-habit/

of my seat. I'm not sure why, but I expected an enlightened, semi-magical, spiritual process only monks might know of to refine one's thought habits. Dandapandi's answer (drum roll please) ... *track it, daily!* That's right, fundamentally identical to THF's process. Only, the system was a bit rudimentary and missing some key components (frequency and minimum success criteria, tracking period, etc.). There was no app or way to chart your progress or compare one month's tracking results against the previous. Dandapandi instructed us on how to develop the "consistent practice" of "concentration." It was to use a calendar and reflect at the end of each day and score yourself using the following criteria/checkboxes: Always, Often, Rarely, Never. (It was very, Ben Franklin-esque). That's it – they (the monks) would go through the month for each behavior or thought habit they were working to improve and check it off at the end of the day.

9) **What is the best way to break a habit?**
Simply put: "A nail is driven out by another nail; habit is overcome by habit."~ Desiderius Erasmus
The best way to break any habit is to *replace* it with a favorable one. Earlier we spoke of habits being associated with other habits or triggers. A ritual is really nothing more than a series of habits. So, for instance, a person's nighttime ritual might be: sit on the couch, drink beer, and eat popcorn while watching TV. This is effectively three habits; watching TV, drinking beer and eating popcorn (four if you want to count sitting on the

couch). A person could tackle this one of two ways: Attempt to alter the entire ritual, or just substitute a healthy snack for the popcorn or a non-alcoholic beer (or tea, water, etc.) for the beverage. It's always important to consider your environment/habitat, which contains many triggers and rituals. As mentioned earlier, you can't spell habitat without first spelling habit. Changing your environment/habitat can be a great catalyst to break a bad habit or forging a new, positive one. However, you may not want to change the TV *and* couch, just the snack or drink, so substitution would be the best method. If you wanted to change the entire ritual, your best course of action would probably be to go into another room at night, or rearrange the furniture, or move the TV, altogether altering the environment!

10) **How does habit differ from virtue?**

Well, it was Aristotle in Nichomachean Ethics who cited, "Ethical virtues are acquired by habituation; they do not arise in us from birth, but we by nature have the capacity to receive and perfect them." Simply put, nobody is born honest. As a virtue, honesty is learned and refined through honesty habits. Recall from the "Meet Benjamin Franklin" chapter that his process to refine his 13 virtues was via his end-of-the-day reflection and tracking.

GOALS

*"People are not lazy. They simply have
impotent goals — that is, goals that do not
inspire them." ~Tony Robbins*

1) Help! I have no idea what my goal should be!

Well, you are not alone, and this is a fairly common
concern. Rather than wonder what your goal should be, try
these two creative mental exercises:

   a) *Ask yourself what your ideal future looks like in, say,
five years.*
A great exercise is to write down a paragraph or
two about the following life categories:
professional, financial, family/social,
lifestyle/home (city) and travel, body, mind,
spiritual, and skills you want to learn. As you
write about each, describe in detail the ideal
situation and how each area would look in five
years. Then, ask yourself if any of these appear
more "pressing" or appealing? Do any excite
you more than the others to go after *now?*

b) The second exercise is to simply ask this question, from earlier in the book, using the power of regret: *"If I were to die tomorrow, what experience would I most regret not having?"*

These are two powerful questions and great goal-starter exercises because they help to give a person a sense of immediate direction!

2) **I know what my goal is, but I have a hard time going after it with a full-time job, school, kids, etc.**

Yes! It seems for most people there are a thousand things competing for their time and attention (as well as money). (Few things are funnier to me than the self-proclaimed productivity expert who has no kids!) Everything changed for me when I began to view productivity and goal achievement as simple math or even physics!

As in: I'm energy. My goal is going to require energy. Therefore, understanding habit (the most efficient form of behavior) and how to craft supportive habits that will carry me efficiently to my goals is the KEY. This is why The Habit Factor has proven to be so helpful to people– it's simply the most efficient process to achieve goals!

3) I know what my goal is, but when I get "real" with myself, I recognize my biggest concern is looking stupid and failing!

It's probably too much of a cliché to assure you that failure is the ONLY path to success, so I'll try a different tact. (BTW, I think it's worth re-reading that sentence.) In fact, this is something I recently heard actor and comedian Jim Carrey say at a commencement ceremony.[29] The fact is, you may think you are comfortable and can't fail where you are, but the reality is, with so much change in the air, the person who doesn't go after their dreams, goals and desires is just as likely to fail where they are – perhaps even more likely, since they won't be passionate about their work. So given that you can (and very likely might) fail at what you *don't* want in life, why wouldn't you attempt to succeed and fail along the way at something you *do* want in life?

4) I have heard that my subconscious mind is far more influential than the conscious mind when it comes to goal achievement. Is this true?

There is no way to know for certain which is more influential. I would agree with many experts who

---

[29] https://www.youtube.com/watch?v=V80-gPkpH6M (specifically minute 11:00-12:00)

suggest that it is the subconscious mind and, if that is the case, consider this: Where do habits reside? In the conscious or the subconscious part of the mind? Bingo!

(For more on mind vs. brain, revisit the chapter, "Welcome to Your Brain, Which Is Not Your Mind" in the Scientific section.)

Motivation & Willpower

"People often say that motivation doesn't last.
Well, neither does bathing – that's why we
recommend it daily." ~Zig Ziglar

1) I've heard that the most important character trait to have is willpower, and it's the greatest predictor of success. Is this true?

First, anytime you hear the word "trait,"[30] particularly associated with a person's character, it has likely been crafted via *habit*. There is plenty of research to support theories that character *traits* like willpower[31] or persistence, resilience /"grit"[32] are key determinants of success. Don't be confused, though! The KEY idea is to know that whatever character trait you wish to develop, it can be and will be *learned*. Nobody is born with willpower and nobody is born persistent! Dr. Stephen Covey once noted that habit lies at the intersection of knowledge, skill and desire.

---

[30] As defined by Merriam Webster: a distinguishing quality of a person's character.
[31] http://www.newyorker.com/magazine/2009/05/18/dont-2
[32] For a graphic on the habits that constitute "Grit", check this out: http://www.thehabitfactor.com/2015/01/if-grit-is-the-key-to-success-what-is-the-key-to-grit-part-iii/

The Habit Factor (book) provides you the <u>Knowledge</u>; if you've ever been persistent or demonstrated willpower even once, and you have the ability to track a behavior, you have the <u>Skills</u> required. However, only YOU know if you have the <u>Desire</u>, which is the *required* third ingredient!

2) **What's the difference between discipline and willpower?**

One of the dictionary definitions for discipline is: "a way of behaving that shows a willingness to obey laws and rules." Then there is Zig Ziglar's definition: "The ability to do what you know you should do when you know you should do it, whether you feel like it or not."

In this sense, discipline and willpower overlap a bit. An essential idea to keep in mind when it comes to willpower is that it too is a derivative of energy. Therefore, often those who act with the most willpower simply have the greatest energy reserves. When your energy reserves are low, willpower lessens. Guess who has more willpower, a person who is hungry or one who just ate lunch? The person who just woke up after a good night's sleep or the person who just came home after a long day?

Knowing that everyone's willpower is likely to wane as they get low on energy, a key realization is to set yourself up for better decision-making when your energy reserves are higher. For instance, packing a salad for later in the day allows you to be prepared and ready to eat that salad instead of grabbing a quick candy bar. Or, making writing your first creative endeavor early, when your energy is higher vs. later in the day when you have no creative energy remaining.

This is precisely why developing the proper, supportive *habits* of your goals and ideals becomes so important. Since by design habits conserve and require less energy, they are a default position, decision, disposition or behavior when your energy reserves are low.

3) **Here's my biggest challenge: All of this makes sense. I get it... I'm just not motivated to go for any of it!**

A couple questions right back at you that may provide clarity about your situation.

1) **Do you regularly work out?** Sounds a bit strange, perhaps, but exercising (even for just 20 minutes) equates to positive emotions. To put it another way, you can't spell emotion without spelling *motion*! *Get moving!* Exercise changes you physiologically and at least three key things happen: self-esteem goes up, energy levels go up, and your body releases mood-enhancing endorphins! Often being stuck or unmotivated is cured by a simple exercise routine. TRACK it for consistency!

2) **How big would a goal have to be to scare you?**
   Can you think of a big-stretch goal that might excite
   or scare you – really challenge you? Recall the Tony
   Robbins quote cited earlier: "Impotent" goals
   equate to a lack of motivation. Whereas big,
   exciting, scary, hairy-type goals result in all sorts of
   emotion that drive action and motivation!

3) **How comfortable are you?** Too much comfort
   creates complacency. Often, altering your
   environment or getting involved in different social
   groups helps to spur motivation and action. When
   we become tied to the familiarity of a common
   environment our senses dull, as do our sensibilities.
   This is why many times even a short vacation is
   known to inspire new ideas and even help create or
   break habits.

Also, I'm sure this will sound a bit cliché, but do what
you can to recognize your "challenge" as an
opportunity. Everyone loses motivation from time to
time, which is natural; the good news is you've
acknowledged it – you're aware. Keep in mind, nothing
that has happened in the past has to have any relevance
toward what you are able to accomplish going forward!
So, just getting back on the horse is half the battle!

Finally, one of the reasons THF is so helpful to people
is it gives them a feeling of success and momentum
right away. I can't tell you how often I hear, "I love

checking off those habits every day!" So, a small streak
— a few days in a row checking off this habit or that one
— and momentum builds. It's unavoidable: Momentum
leads to motivation!

ESSAYS FROM THF CHALLENGE

The Habit Factor Challenge was created a couple of years ago after I received an email from a man named Adrian. Adrian sent me two great images with a very short note. The first image was him crossing the finish line of a marathon, and the other was a screen shot from The Habit Factor app of his goal being stamped "Completed!" (a feature of the app) across the top!

It was short and sweet, and here is what he wrote:

"This was a pretty big deal to me; thanks for the help HF."

I was thrilled! I followed up with Adrian to understand a bit more about the background events leading up to his goal achievement, and he shared that the prior year was unimaginably rough.[33] His email follows:

>>I've gotten into the habit of not telling my backstory for fear that is off putting to some people... but to help you understand the contrast:

Last year was a year in which I had a complete mental break down and as a result of a suicide attempt; I spent 4-5 months in and out of the hospital. I lost a lot

---

[33] A great example of how bringing it back to _now_ matters most, and the Eva story you'll see later in the Conclusion.

of weight--my relationships, home, career and
reputation were turned upside down.

By all means, please share... my new purpose is to be
a shining example of God's love throughout the world.
I welcome anyway that can I can be of help or
inspiration...

Thanks again,
Adrian

Whew! That story still gets me a bit choked up. It's
amazing and powerful and it is simply The Habit Factor in
action – totally *transformational!*

I've experienced it firsthand and I've seen it in action
for years now. The "funny" thing is, it is important to know
that if The Habit Factor is always at work! It's either
working for you or, it's working *against* you![34]

Why not make it work for you?

Famed cosmetics titan Mary Kay once noted that there
are three essential things to help people buy-in and believe
in any service or solution:

Is it easy?	Yes	☑
Does it work?	Yes	☑
Can I do it?	Yes!	☑

---

[34] At the end you will find a terrific poem – a gift to you!

What follows are three fairly recent essays from members of The Habit Factor® Challenge.

Participants were expected to track their supportive habits for four weeks and submit their tracking charts weekly (by a deadline). Part of the challenge was to share the experience in either essay form, video form, or both.

I commend these individuals for their courage to challenge themselves and put these ideas into practice. Their stories inspire me and I'm hopeful they inspire you!

You can find out more about the THF Challenge here: http://www.thehabitfactor.com/win/ and maybe, *someday you'll be up for the challenge too?*

Enjoy!

MY HABIT FACTOR EXPERIENCE

I initially found the Habit Factor after reading a blog on best habit forming apps. I had never thought about achieving my life goals using the power of habit till that blog. I then downloaded all of the apps recommended and found that they were all similar except for the Habit Factor, which allowed both goal tracking and utilizing habits to achieve them. I was hooked after purchasing the book and digesting its content.

It was about then The Habit Factor challenge was issued, so I decided that I would benefit from an external outlet during this beginning phase. I believed that it would make me more committed, and I was right.

So a little about me. I am a recovering drug addict and I also suffer from Bipolar Affective Disorder.[35] So you can imagine I had a host of bad habits and found it extremely difficult to achieve my goals in life due to distraction, procrastination and a lack of routine. I was in an utter state of despair when I read that blog. Then the light turned on and after reading

---

[35] Italics and underlined for effect – not in original essay.

The Habit Factor I saw a way out of the stagnation and constant failing in achieving my goals. It was definitely a life changing experience which has been positively exemplified by The Habit Factor Challenge.

The Habit Factor book made me I realize that to change this cycle of disorder and non-achievement in my life I needed to install new Habits that actively pursued my goals and gave me a routine. Also it showed that instead of concentrating on my bad habits and trying to combat, pursuing these new positive Habits would naturally fill my time, thus negating a lot of the bad habits. This was a new approach for me in defeating my vices, and I have to say that it has worked wonders.

My main goal was to establish a healthy physical and mental regimen which when accomplished would give me the foundation needed to pursue other goals. For the first time in my life I felt able to achieve my goals utilizing The Habit Factor. As I tracked my habits I realized that I was able to focus and this increased momentum. Though not perfect, without The Habit Factor I might have started some, but I guarantee that I would not have pursued them for more than a week. And I would feel defeated and go back to my bad habits. Tracking my habits forced me to address them daily thus regimenting them into a daily routine. And it allowed me to see how I was going and gave positive reinforcement.

So I am extremely grateful to The Habit Factor franchise: the book, the app and the challenge. The book gave me the insights and understanding, the app then allowed me to practically apply this knew knowledge and the challenge motivated me to accomplish these new habits.

Yes, at times it was difficult, especially at the start, but as time moved on and the tracking emphasized these wanna-be habits actually became part and parcel of my daily routine.

For this gift I cannot express my gratitude enough and would highly recommend The Habit Factor to anyone who wants to change their lives for real.

Feiz N. (Australia)

MY HABIT FACTOR EXPERIENCE

I can still remember it like yesterday. It was Tuesday, December 31st and I was listening to an audio teaching from Leadership expert Dr. John Maxwell. On the audio John talked about the importance of having a plan for personal growth. Now when it comes to setting New Year's Resolutions I'm the man for the job. Unfortunately, I come up short every year because I've never had a good system in place for achieving my goals. After finishing the audio I started researching goal setting apps. After reviewing several apps I ran across the Habit Factor App. Two things immediately stood out about the Habit Factor App:

First I was very impressed when I saw that a book had been written to explain the thought process behind properly aligning habits and goals. I started off with the sample first on my Kindle. After reviewing the sample I downloaded the audio book from Audible.com. I listened to the first hour and then I realized that I was missing highlight opportunities, so I went ahead and purchased the e-book. The more I read the book, the more I became excited about what I was reading because Martin kept referencing authors and speakers that I was familiar with, such as Brian Tracy and Napoleon Hill. Secondly, I was excited about being able to participate in the week habit tracking challenge. I knew that if Martin was willing to write a book and hold an accountability challenge, he truly believed that the Habit

Factor could help people achieve their goals. I was excited about having the opportunity to participate.

I will share my Habit Factor experience using the acronym HABIT.

H – Habit Factor

The H is for the Habit Factor App. The Habit Factor is an amazing app that is really easy to use. One of the things that I love about this app is the simplicity of it and the fact that I spend less than 5 minutes a day in the app. I noticed a couple of things that I believe would make the app easier to use. 1- It would be great if the app allowed for multiple profiles to be created. I'm planning on using the worksheets to track reading habits for my two oldest sons (5 & 7). Another area for improvement would be to be able to share data across devices.

A – Accountability

The A is for Accountability. The number 1 reason why I signed up for the Habit Factor challenge is because I wanted to put myself in an environment where I could be accountable for my actions. As part of the challenge I was required to submit the results of my weekly habit tracking. I have to admit that there were plenty of nights where I stayed up past midnight in order to complete my daily habits because I wanted to be accountable.

B – Begin with the End in Mind

In the book the 7 Habits of Effective People, one of the habits that Steven Covey suggests is to Begin with the End in Mind. So the B in our acronym stands for 'Begin with the End in Mind'. This concept works great using the Habit Factor app. You first identify your goal as if it has already been achieved and then you work backwards by identifying the habits that are required to accomplish that goal. When I read about this concept in the book, I immediately started thinking about other successful people and the habits that they must have developed to achieve their success. I looked into John Maxwell and I found where he talked about the 5 habits that he uses everyday (Reading, Filing, Thinking, Writing, and Questioning). After I set my personal goal to read 52 books in 2014, I searched online to find other people that had accomplished this to discover their habits.

I – Inspiration

The I is for Inspiration. I had lots of inspiration for doing the challenge as well as staying consistent towards my goals. A big inspiration is the iPad prize. As the sole provider for a family of five I'd probably never spend the money on an iPad, but I do have the discipline to go after my goals. The late Jim Rohn said that if you have enough reasons you accomplish anything. In the book's forward, Roz Savage wrote, "If you have a big enough reason 'Why', you will always be able to find your 'How'."

One of the great things about the Habit Factor app is that when you are setting up your goals you have the opportunity to enter one or more reasons why the goal is important to you. In addition, as you are setting up your habits you have the opportunity to add additional reasons for each habit.

To help maintain my motivation during the challenge, I created a video consisting of images and quotes that reminded me of what I'm attempting to accomplish in 2014. I am passionate about personal growth and becoming what God designed me to be.

T – Tracking

The T is for Tracking. In the Habit Factor book Martin Grunburg says that we don't get what we want; we get what we track. With the Habit Factor app habit tracking can be done with a simple click. In fact, it takes less time for me to track my habits using this app than it would to open up Excel on my PC. Another benefit of this tracking is that you can run reports to see how you are progressing towards your goals. The best thing about the tracking feature is that it doesn't contain room for excuses. Either you did it or you didn't. Like I mentioned before, I love the simplicity of this app.

So How Has It Worked?

So how is it working for me? Over the last 5 weeks since I've been using the Habit Factor app I have read 5 books and I have been more consistent towards my personal growth goal of reading 52 books and listening to over 1,000 audios this year. Thanks to the Habit Factor Philosophy I feel more confident that I can achieve any goal that I set as long as I'm willing to identify and track the proper habits.

Conclusion

Napoleon Hill said that, "You are where you are and what you are because of your established habits of thought and deed." I'm looking forward to sitting down on December 31, 2014 and running my habit report over the entire year and seeing how my consistency has helped me hit my goals. Napoleon Hill also talked about developing the Habit of going the Extra Mile, so I decided to go the extra mile by continuing to track my goals and creating a speech in addition to this essay.

Thanks for the opportunity to be accountable!

Michael P., Ohio

Here are two videos that I created for the Habit Factor Challenge and to assist me with maintaining my consistency.

Habit Factor Experience Playlist:
http://www.youtube.com/playlist?list=PLbBu6nkpFqGaG2-OqZbc3LBVDuSM0YAcz
Vision Video/Mind Movie
http://www.youtube.com/watch?v=DUhT7ZkLaKY
Habit Factor Experience Speech (Given to 17 people at a Toastmasters meeting)
http://www.youtube.com/watch?v=a8KHmXoq_kU

THE HABIT FACTOR EXPERIENCE

My father is 80 years old. He has Alzheimer's.

His father died at 84 years old – of Alzheimer's.

I have an overall life goal: Don't die of Alzheimer's.

I have done all kinds of research on how to avoid Alzheimer's. There are four things I can do:

Avoid having a family history. I can't do anything about that one.

Keep my mind active. Given my job, I really have to do this – so it happens automatically.

Keep my body active. This was one area where I need help.

Manage my diet. There is increasing evidence that the foods we eat can help avoid Alzheimer's, or move us toward it.

Knowing my family history – and knowing the research – you would think that I would just naturally do everything I can to decrease my odds of Alzheimer's. I would exercise. I would manage my diet.

I don't. I try ... but I don't do it.

So when a friend of mine recommended The Habit Factor I figured, "Why not?" I signed up for the trial.

My initial focus was primarily on my health – with the overall goal of avoiding Alzheimer's.

I wanted to get more exercise, and I wanted to do something for my diet, so I set up the following habits:

1. Drink 8 glasses of water a day. This would mean less coffee, less diet soda, and more water. It wouldn't be easy, but I knew it to be the right decision.

2. Get 30 minutes of exercise per day. To make tracking easy, I decided to use my Fitbit. At the end of the day, when I logged on to the Habit Tracker, it was easy – look at the Fitbit. If it showed 30 minutes of exercise, I completed it. If not, get up and get moving!

Early on I realized that I would need help: Before the official tracking period started I one day looked and realized I was 3 glasses of water and 15 minutes of exercise short. I had to get my checkmarks, so I chugged some water. The 15 minutes shortly followed, as did quick trips to the bathroom all night long.

I then read more of the Habit Factor book. I realized I needed to do something to make my drink choice, and my exercise, literally a "no brainer." When I thought about the ways to be healthy I realized that one (keep my mind active) happened automatically. I didn't need to even think about it. My job requires reading, thought, analysis, etc.

I needed something similar for my diet habit and my exercise habit.

After reading about the conscious and unconscious parts of my brain, I realized that if I did things right, I could make the 30 minutes of exercise and 8 glasses of water automatic.

I came up with the following ideas:

For the water I bought a case of bottled water and put it underneath my desk. Now when I reached to the area that used to store Diet Coke, or energy drinks, I grabbed a 16 ounce bottle of water. Within two days I was automatically getting my water. Within a week I was loving the taste of water as a drink.

For the 30 minutes' worth of high active exercise, I thought back to my younger days. When my wife and I were first married we lived in a more urban area – everyone walked fast. We all felt like we were always had somewhere to get to in a hurry. When we visited our parents in the rural area I was frustrated with how slow people walked. I would forever be walking up people's back.

Later in life we moved to the rural area. When I thought about it I realized I had let my walking become "rural." I was walking slowly. Meandering. I wondered – could it be as simple as training myself to walk faster from meeting to meeting? From my office to lunch? From my car to the office and back? Just. Walk. Faster. Would that work?

I started walking faster. Within a week it was second nature. Sure enough, I was getting my 30 minutes in automatically!

Both of those habits were started because of the Habit Factor application. I had to get my check mark at the end of the day. The review at the end of the day is the engine that makes this work. Knowing I will need to check off (or not check off) a habit motivates me to first practice the habit, and then find ways to make that habit happen automatically.

As I progressed I added new goals and new supporting habits. The idea was to find habits that support my overall goal – and then train myself to make the habits an automatic part of my life.

I have done this both in my health area, as well as my personal goal area. I have had success in both areas, but by far the one most important to me is health.

Now that I've made my first two goals automatic, I can move on to bigger and better things. The next phase is to replace my factory made snacks with healthy snacks. Once again, I make them readily available. When I reach for a snack, instead of chips I will find a banana, or some berries, or maybe some 70+% cocoa dark chocolate. It's working! (Especially when I eat the dark chocolate.)

Is this a great improvement in my life? Absolutely. Will this be enough to avoid Alzheimer's? Maybe yes, maybe no. But in the end, regardless of what happens I will be able to look at my family, and look at myself in the mirror and say "I did everything I could to avoid Alzheimer's and live life to the fullest." This app and book have helped put me on the path to do that.

Phil B., Ohio

BOOK BONUS

"We make a living by what we get.
We make a life by what we give."
~Winston S. Churchill

For me, the definition of success, in essence, is *creating your ideal future*. In order to create your ideal future, you must know how to set and achieve goals *consistently* -- there is no other way.

To test this notion, please think of any "great" person or personal hero and ask:

1) Did they create their ideal life? Sure, there were many hardships, obstacles, etc., but did they fully actualize what they were trying to BEcome?

2) Did they set and achieve goals, habitually?

3) Did their habits (which forged their character) support those goals? Were their habits fully aligned with the goals and the people they intended to become – and ultimately became?

The answer, in every case, must be YES!

To that end, The Habit Factor methodology is the most efficient and effective goal-achievement strategy that exists. Its principles are timeless and its practices are proven.

Parenthetically, have you ever noticed how *any* self-help program will plead with you to "give their product, service or program a try for at least 21 days"? Or maybe they'll give you a "30 day challenge" so you are committed to trying it for "X" number of days.

What are they trying to get you to do? Correct! They're hopeful that you'll develop the *habit* of using their tools, service or program. Unfortunately, in many cases what they haven't done is teach you about <u>habit</u>, why it exists and how you can intentionally craft supportive habits *and* align them to your goals.[36]

To that end, I'm inviting YOU to visit (*right now, why delay your greatness?*) <u>www.thehabitfactor.com/jumpstarter</u> and gain access to new tools and resources to help launch your own successful transformation.

Remember, *ALL* self-improvement relies upon a single, all-powerful force – and it is HABIT.

Please consider this "jumpstarter" a sincere gift and a Thank You for your investment of time, energy and attention. We will continue to update the list of free tools and resources to accelerate your efforts as you *Create Your Ideal Future!*

<u>NOTE</u>: The referenced Book Bonus page (link, next page) will also be updated, so check back for new free bonuses and discounts – again, as my sincere thank you.

---

[36] Incredibly, this is now a growing trend today (educating people about habit), which was my goal when this book was first published in 2010.

Book Bonus! *Free* **Month of THF ProCloud app**
Use the new THF ProCloud app and sync *unlimited active* habits and goals to the cloud and across devices[37].

Two ways to receive:

1) Simply email sales@equilibrium-ent.com **with your book receipt,** (attached or screen-shot) **Subject Title: FREE MONTH PROCLOUD** (all caps), *and we'll email you a personalized promo code!* OR,

2) Scan the below code/click the below link to register!

http://thehabitfactor.com/bookbonus

Be sure to check back for other bonuses, tools and updates!

---

[37] The FREE version of the portal allows for up to 1 Active Goal and 3 Active habits to track. Also, depending upon when you read this, the portal may not yet be available. Syncing currently only between iOS devices – Android in the works.

Epilogue

Before enlightenment, chop wood and carry water.
After enlightenment, chop wood and carry water.
~Zen Proverb

The other day my daughter Eva, who is seven years old, asked her mother, "Mommy, when is the future created?"

This, it turned out, was one gem of a question – an unintentional, real-life Zen Koan that my wife shared with me. She said, rather perplexed, "I wasn't sure what to tell her." (A Zen Koan is a seemingly contradictory and/or nonsensical statement/question that can be answered only with a new and altered perception/perspective. Answers tend not to come into view until the student has shifted her perception and become receptive and aware; hence, the classic Zen proverb, "When the student is ready, the master appears.")

I realized that I had no response either to my daughter's question. Stumped, I decided that I would sleep on it. *"When is the future created?"* I kept asking myself. What a great question. I even posted it on Facebook to see what my friends thought. One friend suggested I tell Eva, "Tomorrow! Tell her the future is created tomorrow."

Forty-eight hours later the answer hit me:
<u>NOW</u>!

That's it! The future is created now! There is no tomorrow and there is no yesterday. The only moment we all have is *now*. I'm sure we all recognize this on some level, but how many of us have contemplated its significance? It is so significant, in fact, a great Zen Master, Sheng-ts'an, once proclaimed, "No tomorrow. No today. No yesterday." There can only be *NOW*. Thank you, Eva and Sheng-ts'an.

Such an awakening should provide everyone a tremendous reprieve. Reflect on that for a moment; it makes literally no difference how "bad" yesterday, last week, last year or even today *was*, not even the last 10 years or 10 seconds – none! The future (your future) is created *now*. And now, I remind you, is where habit is listening very intently, recording your present energies (thoughts and actions) right at *this moment*.

My Goal/Why I Wrote This

"Kids are 25% of our population and 100% of our future."
~Anonymous

So here is my big goal and vision for this book. In fact, this is my "Why?" and it probably makes sense to share it, since you have taken the time to read it (thank you). The answer is, I "had to" write this book. My main goal is to help young adults, even high school-age kids, recognize that regardless of their circumstance, with The Habit Factor working *for* them, they *will* achieve their goals.

There is so much noise and there are so many
distractions between TV, the Internet and video games; too
many young adults come out of college and especially high
school completely confused about how to channel their
energy. Most have no idea how to set or achieve their goals.
Schools are designed to prepare students for a life of
service, productivity and achievement, and given what has
been disclosed within these pages, I'm confident that such
an understanding of the subject of HABIT would greatly
serve *our collective future*. In fact, I strongly believe that
everything there is to know about habit (the related science,
nature and even theories, much like any other scientific
theories and languages that are taught in school) ought to be
learned by our children *now*.

Habit is the fertile ground and well spring of success.
Yet, ask any young adult or teenager to describe habit and
you'll likely hear, "A habit is like smoking or taking drugs."
You're unlikely to hear, "Habit is my special weapon of
achievement. If I choose and forge my habits diligently and
wisely, I will achieve nearly any goal I desire and, ultimately,
realize the lifestyle of my dreams."

CONCLUSION

So the time has come for *you* "to chop wood and carry
water." To do the little things and do them well, *consistently*
with your newfound perspective. It's important to know
that such enlightenment changes everything and yet changes
nothing. That is, since the only things we can control are
our thoughts, enlightenment is exclusively a mental shift

where the external world appears to have changed, but the only change has been within.

Even with a complete appreciation for the magnificence of habit, hard work and diligence are required. Just because Roz clearly understood the profound importance of habit, it did not allow her to sit back and reach the other side of the ocean without a consistency of effort!

The Habit Factor assures us that the hard work will get easier, *over time*. The Habit Factor isn't a "secret" and it isn't a shortcut; it is an awareness and an appreciation. Such an enlightened perspective helps to remove doubt and diminish fear, leaving only the complete assurance that the same powerful force that has been applied by the greatest achievers of all time is now entirely at your disposal.

Use it wisely.

As you might expect, my goal above (app screenshot) was to "Complete Book THF!" accomplished using The Habit Factor app, tracking my habits!!

ANOTHER FORCE... ANOTHER BOOK?

> Hey Martin, I'm Brandon's younger brother. He told me to
> contact you! I just finished reading The Habit Factor, it's
> amazing! I'm sharing it with everyone I can to spread the ideas
> around; it's really cool stuff and different from anything I've read
> before. Let me know when you publish other books so I can
> read them as well! ~Cheers! Brett

I'm very pleased to let you (and Brett) know that there
is, in fact, another book in the works. And, like habit, when
understood and applied intentionally and with purpose,
anyone's achievements and productivity *must accelerate* at a
terrific pace. *Here's the best part: The two forces work in perfect
tandem – as if by design.*

I'm not sure I could have appreciated this force (and its
respective role) until now – *after* The Habit Factor, and the
same may be true for you. Many people might even argue
that *this* particular force is more powerful and influential
than habit, and that without its benefit, habit loses much of
its value and impact.

This timeless force also works its magic on both the
physical and invisible planes. It's known to inspire greatness
and world-class performances of the highest level, and at
the same time it could cause a person's professional and
personal ruin.

It's the very same force that moves the pistons in your
car, pushes trains of impossible weight across the country
and is at least partially responsible for putting a man on the
moon (both technologically and motivationally speaking).

The philosophies in this new book completely envelop themselves around those contained within The Habit Factor, making this new work, truly, its perfect complement. My friends, welcome to **The Pressure Paradox!**

(Short preview follows...)

From the chapter currently titled "DAVE"

… As I rode my bicycle home, I kept thinking about what he'd said as I walked out the door.

"You've always been great at that."

"What?" I replied, holding the door and looking back.

"Your ability to commit – to stick to a deadline."

It's a bit ironic now as I write this, because as I recall we were discussing *his* book – the one that had been in the works for months and now, as it turns out, years.

Then it hit me.

Regardless of any past achievement, I didn't have to look too far to find a sort of culminating episode – often a deadline and sometimes a performance date, as with a triathlon. There were also self-imposed deadlines as with the book, developing apps, starting companies, introducing products or services, etc.

Wait, I can hear you now, "Having a deadline to enhance productivity or accelerate creativity is hardly a new revelation." Correct! In fact, it's often a requirement – a critical component in any productivity puzzle and one that should not go without notice.

However, if we look a little deeper something far more mysterious and significant emerges, something that goes beyond each and every individual deadline.

Behind, within and around every deadline is a force much greater than the deadline itself – a supernatural force responsible for nearly every great invention, idea and achievement throughout history.

This force has propelled many of the greatest achievers to perform at their highest level. And, paradoxically, it's a force most often responsible for demoralizing, destroying and debilitating those who do not have a proper awareness and understanding of its nature.

It is *pressure – an omnipotent force that permeates our lives. It has been with us since our birth and will be with us until our last breath.*

And, interestingly, the physical laws of pressure have been identified centuries ago by many of the greatest physicists and mathematicians throughout history. What appears to have been missed, though, is how quite literally the laws transcend the physical universe and invade the non-physical – the realm of the unseen.

Deadlines are effective because they create *pressure.* However, that statement begets some new, larger questions, such as:

What is pressure? How does it originate, and how might we apply these physical laws toward our own productivity and performance?

We might even ask, "Why does pressure exist?"

Recall Aristotle's quote from the beginning: "... is to seek for the second kind of principle, that from which comes the beginning of the change."

"...that from which comes the beginning of the change."

Fascinating.

That is what we're all after, isn't it? "The beginning of the change."

I'm sure you realize a significant case can be made that the Universe itself doesn't even exist without the vital contribution of pressure?

So, if science's best guess about universal creation, "The Big Bang" theory, is even remotely close, then we can thank our very existence to, of all things, pressure.

A great rock-and-roll band from the '70s, The Doobie Brothers, produced the classic song "Long Train Running (Without Love)," which has the chorus, "Without love, where would you be now?"

We might all very well ask the same question about pressure. Sing it, "[Without pressure,] where would you be now?"

It's a bit captivating to view pressure in this new light – **as an active participant in the creation of <u>all</u> existence, a giver of life and as purely a creative force responsible for you, the reader.** *Pressure may be the single greatest creative force in our universe.*

So you might be wondering, then, "When did we ever learn this in school?"

Who teaches us this?

I'm fairly sure there wasn't a "Pressure 101" class in high school that I could have attended or, at the very least, ditched.

(End Preview... TBR, Summer 2015)

ACKNOWLEDGEMENTS

"The great use of life is to spend it for
something that will outlast it."
~William James

I'm pleased to report that what you hold in your hands is an artifact of its own thesis. As I've worked on this manuscript for more than three years now, there have been many projects and priorities competing for my time along the way. True to theme, I have remained steadfast to complete this pet project. Admittedly, there were many days the successful outcome of this book seemed to be in question and often my "Target" of writing for just "20 minutes a day" (at the beginning), or later, "one hour a day," appeared to produce little headway; it was my faith in the process that encouraged me to remain optimistic.

Given the amount of time that went into this manuscript and the countless people I leaned on for support and encouragement, as well as inspiration, it's my honor to share the names of those whom I'm able to recall, and to all whom I may have forgotten, a sincere thank you!

Many thanks to my best men: Mark Levy, Stephen Hodge and Richard Grunburg. To my creative and intelligent collaborators, Gretchen (my wife, who's had to listen to me ramble about this stuff for years), Dave Allen and Jordan Taylor. To my tri training partner Chris Laden, thanks for pushing me up those long hills. To "The Rock," a brilliant group of entrepreneurs: Brendan Hayes, Wayne Levy, Jon Carder, Brian Moadelli, Dylan Steer, Derek Preston, Sarah Hardwick and Ricardo Cardenas. Your support for The Habit Factor book and methodology and related insights has been essential. Thanks too, to our former members David Steel, Scott Bertone, Paul Reynolds, Derek Baggerly, Mark Hoffman, Reid Carr, Greg Barry and Shaun Alger (*Shaun, appreciate the introduction*), and to all EO SD: a truly remarkable group of entrepreneurs and business leaders. To Glenn Arnold and his head's-up recommendation.

To Paul Palmer, CEO, Big Brothers and Big Sisters San Diego, your remarkable leadership has helped to improve the lives of thousands of at-risk kids throughout San Diego! To Steve Williams and Matt Spathas: You are both consummate leaders and mentors.

To "The Band": Scott Fink, William Fleming and Jeremy Ognall, your friendship and support over the many years is responsible for so many great memories. To Martha Cullimore, Lance Kling and Eric Berman, your encouragement and introductions were always so critical and well timed. To Mike Smith, who was always there at the Manhattan pier to show support and provide a crash pad post race.

To the many great authors who've provided guidance and support along the way, including Brian Tracy, Michael Gerber, Anthony Smith, Chip Conley, Tammy Greenwood and Vern Harnish. Special thanks to Roz Savage: You're an inspiration and a modern-day superhero.

Special thanks, too, to the best business partners and mentors any man could be lucky enough to work with, Edmon Hagee and Duke Ayers, and their lovely brides Christine and Colleen. As we are great fans of the late John Wooden, I will share one of his favorite quotes from Cervantes: "The journey is better than the Inn." Thanks, too, to our remarkable C3 Networx and Home2Office teams and of course our wonderful clients.

To my parents: You surrounded me with perhaps the greatest habits of all; love and encouragement. To my brothers, Richard, Anders and my "little" brother Mark, I'm indebted to you all for the many important lessons. To the in-laws, your undying love and support remains a mystery to me: John, Lisa, Richard and Nancy Lingham, and, of course, Margaret – you will always be remembered. Thanks so much for raising the most remarkable woman and now, phenomenal mother.

To the ocean (yes, the ocean.) Your abundant supply of energy, creativity, beauty and joy could never be replaced.

To my wife Gretchen: Simply put, you are the most beautiful and brilliant woman I've ever known.

This work is a product of your collective friendship, support and love. Thank you all!

[Who Am I?]

I am your constant companion.
I am your greatest helper or heaviest burden.
I will push you onward or drag you down to failure.

I am completely at your command.
Half of the things you do you might as well turn over to me
and I will do them – quickly and correctly.

I am easily managed – you must be firm with me.
Show me exactly how you want something done
and after a few lessons, I will do it automatically.

I am the servant of all great people,
and alas, of all failures as well.
Those who are great, I have made great.
Those who are failures, I have made failures.

I am not a machine though
I work with the precision of a machine
plus the intelligence of a person.

You may run me for profit or run me for ruin –
it makes no difference to me.

Take me, train me, be firm with me, and
I will place the world at your feet.

Be easy with me and I will destroy you.
Who am I?

I am Habit

(Author Unknown)

End Notes:

---

[i] Martin, Neale. *The 95% of Behavior Marketers Ignore.* FT Press, December, 2009, and Wood, Wendy, Quinn, Jeffrey M. and Kashy, Deborah A. *Habits in Everyday Life: Thought, Emotion, and Action.* Journal of Personality and Social Psychology, 2002, Vol. 83, No. 6, 1281–1297.
<http://college.usc.edu/wendywood/research/documents/Wood.Quinn.Kash y.2002.pdf>

[ii] Duhigg, Charles. *Warning: Habits May Be Good for You.* New York Times. July 13, 2008.
http://www.nytimes.com/2008/07/13/business/13habit.html?pagewanted=1& _r=1

[iii] Department of Neuroendocrinology, University of Lübeck, Germany. *Odor Cues During Slow-Wave Sleep Prompt Declarative Memory.* Consolidation Science 9 March 2007: Vol. 315. no. 5817, pp. 1426 – 1429
http://www.sciencemag.org/cgi/content/abstract/315/5817/1426

[iv] PBS FrontLine® *The Persuaders.*
http://www.pbs.org/wgbh/pages/frontline/shows/persuaders/interviews/rap aille.html >YouTube: : Clotaire Rapaille Reptilian Marketing"

[v] Martin, Neale. *The 95% of Behavior Marketers Ignore.* FT Press, December, 2009.

[vi] Truth Campaign, "Rat Man." August 1, 2010.
http://www.youtube.com/watch?v=HiwWz5RJ8zE

[vii] Championship Stress: Ron Artest; post game interview: July, 14, 2010.
http://www.youtube.com/watch?v=vMCeZK3OiKM

[viii] Sokolove, Michael. *How a Soccer Star is Made.* New York Times. June 2, 2010.
http://www.nytimes.com/2010/06/06/magazine/06Soccer-t.html

^{ix}: Wikipedia "Goal Setting" modified August 11, 2010. http://en.wikipedia.org/wiki/Goal_setting

^x PBS "Benjamin Franklin: An Extraordinary Life." *An Electric Mind.* February 1, 2010. http://www.pbs.org/benfranklin/

^{xi} Gladwell, Malcolm. *Outliers: The Story of Success.* Little, Brown and Company, November 2008.

Images and Illustrations:

Google Search. "Why do habits exist?" Screen Shot. | Equilibrium
Limbic System. Brain limbicsystem.jpg | Wikimedia Commons | Nathanael Bar-Aur L. | Governmental source: http://teens.drugabuse.gov/mom/mom_opi5.asp
Brain Lobes. | Wikimedia Commons | Mysid | Governmental source: http://commons.wikimedia.org/wiki/File:Gray728.svg
Hippocampus. | Wikimedia Commons | Derivative work: Looie496 | April 19, 2008 source: http://en.wikipedia.org/wiki/File:Gray739-emphasizing-hippocampus.png
DNA Chemical Structure. | Wikimedia Commons | Madprime | March 28, 2007: http://en.wikipedia.org/wiki/File:DNA_chemical_structure.svg
M83 Galaxy. | NASA |
Low Pressure Storm. | Wikimedia Commons | Brian0918 | NASA | November, 2005 http://commons.wikimedia.org/wiki/File:Low_pressure_system_over_Iceland.jpg
Nautilus Shell. | Wikimedia Commons | Chris 73 | January 22, 2009: http://en.wikipedia.org/wiki/File:NautilusCutawayLogarithmicSpiral.jpg
Sunflower. | Wikimedia Commons | Date=2006 | Author=L. Shyamal | http://en.wikipedia.org/wiki/File:Helianthus_whorl.jpg
Habit communication via subconscious. | Grunburg
My Wife & My Mother In Law. | Wikimedia Commons | Date=2006 | Author=Bryan Derksen | http://commons.wikimedia.org/wiki/File:My_Wife_and_My_Mother-In-Law_(Hill).svg

Bibliography and Additional Readings

A detailed list of supportive materials, including; articles, Web sites, research papers and even multimedia links are listed by section below.

INTRODUCTION

James, William. "Talks to Teachers on Psychology," 2/1/2008.
    <http://www.gutenberg.org/files/16287/16287-h/16287-h.htm>.
    July, 2005
Habit and Goals: Wikipedia Entry, "Habit (Psychology)," September 29,
    2010. <http://en.wikipedia.org/wiki/Habit_(psychology)>
Savage, Roz. *Rowing the Atlantic: Lessons Learned on the Open Ocean.* Simon
    & Shuster, October, 2009.
Hill, Napoleon. *Think and Grow Rich.* Fawcett Crest Book, 1960.
Hill, Napoleon and W. Stone. *Success Through a Positive Mental Attitude.*
    Pocket, 2007.
Assaraf, John. (YouTube), "Law of Attraction - *Why the law of attraction
    won't work in a positive way for 99.9% of people.*" July 10, 2010
    <http://www.youtube.com/watch?v=KMtSMcLVl-4>
Walker, Brian Brown. *The Tao Te Ching of Lao Tzu.* St Martin's Griffin,
    November 1996.
Aristotle, 384BCE – 322 BCE. Nicomachean Ethics. August 1, 2008.
    <http://www.gutenberg.org/ebooks/8438>

THE SCIENTIFIC

PBS.org. "Changing The Mind."
    http://www.pbs.org/saf/1101/index.html
Paul D. MacLean. Wikipedia.
    http://en.wikipedia.org/wiki/Paul_D._MacLean
Dr. Ann Graybiel. MIT. http://web.mit.edu/bcs/graybiel-
    lab/people/ann_graybiel.html
Dr. Fred Goodwin. Transcript from Infinite Mind: Habit. June 9, 2006.
    http://web.mit.edu/bcs/graybiel-lab/news/Habit.pdf
Duhigg, Charles. *Warning: Habits May Be Good for You.* New York Times.
    July 13, 2008.
Wood, Wendy, Quinn, Jeffrey M. and Kashy, Deborah A. "Habits in
    Everyday Life: Thought, Emotion, and Action." Journal of
    Personality and Social Psychology, 2002, Vol. 83, No. 6, 1281–
    1297.
http://college.usc.edu/wendywood/research/documents/Wood.Quin.
    Kashy.2002.pdf
N.H. Azrin and R.G. Nunn. *Habit Reversal: A method of eliminating nervous
    habits and tics.* November 1973 Behavior Research and Therapy.
    Volume 11. Number 4.

George Lakoff and Mark Johnson. *Philosophy in the Flesh: The Embodied Mind and Its Challenge to Western Thought.* Basic Books, December, 1999.

Maltz, Maxwell. *Psycho-Cybernetics, A New Way to Get More Out of Life.* Pocket, August 1989.

THE ESOTERIC

Russell, Bertrand. *What I Believe.* Routledge, February 2004.

Mullis, Kary. *Dancing Naked in the Mind Field.* Vintage, January, 2000.

Livio, Mario. *The Golden Ratio: The Story of PHI, The World's Most Astonishing Number.* Broadway, September, 2003.

Fanning, Philip Ashley. *Isaac Newton and the Transmutation of Alchemy: An Alternative View of the Scientific Revolution.* North Atlantic Books, July, 2009.

Jung, C.G. *The Archetypes and the Collective Unconscious.* Volume 9, Part I. Bollingen, August 1981.

Gladwell, Malcolm. *Outliers: The Story of Success.* Little, Brown and Company, November 2008.

THE INTERSECTION

Harnish, Verne. *The Rockefeller Habits: What You Must Do to Increase the Value of Your Growing Firm.* Select Books, January 2010.

Park, Alice. *The Brain: Marketing to your Mind.* TIME, January 19, 2007. http://www.time.com/time/magazine/article/0,9171,1580370,00. html

Allen, James (1864 – 1912). *As a Man Thinketh.* Gutenberg.org . http://www.gutenberg.org/ebooks/4507 . October 1, 2003.

Sokolove, Michael. *How a Soccer Star is Made.* New York Times. June 2, 2010. http://www.nytimes.com/2010/06/06/magazine/06Soccer-t.html

APPLICATION

Savage, Roz. *Rowing the Atlantic: Lessons Learned on the Open Ocean.* Simon & Shuster, October, 2009.

S.M.A.R.T. Goals. Wikipedia | September 19, 2010. http://en.wikipedia.org/wiki/SMART_criteria

Franklin, Benjamin. *The Autobiography of Benjamin Franklin.* Gutenberg.org http://www.gutenberg.org/files/20203/20203-h/20203-h.htm. February 1, 2008.

Marden, Orison Swett. (1848 – 1924). *The Miracle of Right Thought.* 1910. http://www.archive.org/details/cu31924029125495

Bettger, Frank. *How I Raised Myself from Failure to Success in Selling.* Fireside, April 1992.

Covey, Stephen R. *The 7 Habits of Highly Effective People.* Free Press November 2004.

Frankl, Viktor E. *Man's Search for Meaning.* Beacon Press, June 2006.

NOTES

NOTES

NOTES

NOTES

NOTES

NOTES

Made in the USA
Middletown, DE
12 February 2021